Ship

SHIP

SHIPWRECKED

WRECKED

THE FULL STORY

Jo Foley

First published in February 2001 by Channel 4 Books, an imprint of Macmillan
Publishers Ltd, 25 Eccleston Place, London SW1W 9NF, Basingstoke and Oxford.

Associated companies throughout the world.

www.macmillan.com

ISBN 0 7522 1937 5

A CIP catalogue record for this book is available from the British Library.

Designed and typeset by Janice Mather at Ben Cracknell Studios
Photography by Shauna Minoprio
Colour reproduction by Blackjacks
Printed and bound by Mackays of Chatham plc

RDF MEDIA

This book accompanies the television series *Shipwrecked*, made by RDF Media.com Ltd
for Channel 4.

Executive producer: David Frank

Series Producer: Shauna Minoprio

ACKNOWLEDGEMENTS

Jo Foley would like to thank Shauna Minoprio and
David Frank at RDF Media, Alice Mayhall, also at RDF, for her
unending patience, Rob Dimery for his help and editor
Gillian Christie for her constant reassurance.

CONTENTS

WHO WILL IT BE?

Imagine a perfect South Sea island – white sandy beaches, warm blue seas, miles from anywhere. Imagine its wooded interior, full of lush vegetation and tropical plants, papaya trees and coconut palms. And then imagine being washed up on this island thousands of miles from home with only a few possessions and some basic skills, and being left to fend for yourself. Fortunately (or unfortunately, depending on your point of view) you won't be alone: sixteen strangers will be with you. This isn't a fairy story – this is what really happened when the cast of *Shipwrecked* series two arrived on the Tongan island of Nuku to be filmed for television. These seventeen strangers would be expected to build shelters, fish and forage for food, cook and look after themselves with no help from anyone else. The nearest inhabited island was a good two-hour boat trip away, while the nearest major city – Auckland in New Zealand – was some 2,000 kilometres off, as the crow flies.

Over 20,000 applicants answered the advertisement asking for volunteers for the second series. The ad went out on Channel 4 as the first series drew to a close, and it would appear that nothing the programme showed – no amount of hardship, sickness, in-fighting, sunburn, diarrhoea, loathing, loneliness, abandonment or mosquitoes – was enough to prevent huge numbers of people from wanting to make that experience their own. On national television, of course.

Within days, the offices of the programme's production company, RDF Media, were awash with mail bags, computers

were struggling to cope with e-mails and the phones wouldn't stop ringing. Extra staff were drafted in to cope with the applications – and all to find fourteen people (plus another three from elsewhere – more about them later) eager to give up over two months of their lives to see if they could survive in an unfamiliar tropical paradise.

Within a couple of weeks, the 20,000 were whittled down to 1,000 hopefuls, who were then asked to submit videos of themselves so that the production team could begin sifting out the personalities they needed. 'It was almost like casting a drama,' producer Shauna Minoprio explained. 'We needed real characters who interacted with each other. They needed to be original and sparky as well as looking relaxed on camera.' They also needed to be between the ages of eighteen and twenty-five, and be both geographically and socially from a mixture of backgrounds. The applications turned into an open season for show-offs as well as the ambitious, but it wasn't just the most professional-looking videos that took their stars through to the next round. One applicant with no hope of begging, borrowing or even stealing a video camera used all her persuasive charm to get the manager of her local camera shop to take one of his display models into the street and film her. 'It was truly terrible,' revealed one of the production team, 'but the idea was so original and ingenious that we had to choose her.'

Others headed for the great outdoors, to beaches, farmland and countryside to make their own videos. A few chose to involve a lavatory, stripping or dressing up in everything from blonde wigs to furry penguin outfits – anything to get noticed. One posed as an urban terrorist and tried to capture a pigeon in Trafalgar Square – practice that might well come in handy when, half a world away, they needed to catch a chicken for supper. They pleaded and pouted, exposed their leadership skills

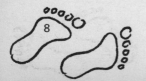

8

and their flies. One girl shook her substantial assets for tr camera and one of the boys rapped. All were desperate to impress, make their mark and get the chance to go on the adventure of a lifetime.

In front of cameras, supported by boyfriends, girlfriends, workmates, families or just a sideboard, they extolled their many virtues. 'I'm easy to get on with'; 'I'm laid-back'; 'I'm of sound mind and love animals'; 'I'm healthy'; 'I'll keep the viewers hooked with my smile'; 'I'm outgoing, resourceful and humorous'; 'I can cook, build, sew'; 'I would be a great agony aunt'; 'I want to be scared'; 'I want to be a kid again'. The reasons were as diverse as the applicants, but every one of them was desperate to be chosen. Everyone wanted their fifteen minutes of fame.

And would it all be worth it? 'Yes, yes and yes!' was the enthusiastic response from one of the original shipwreckees, Will Deed. 'It was the most fantastic experience and we were all lucky to be chosen. It was life-enhancing and wonderful and I would do it all over again. Even a year later I still think of it and want to go back.'

And the key to everything, he explained, was the people: 'You're in a strange place with strange people and you have to survive. But it is the people who make the difference. You realize after a few weeks that you can't get on with everyone, and you gradually start training yourself to ignore them. Now, it's easy at home if you don't like someone – you just don't see them. But on a small island with a handful of people, the only way to survive is to learn to ignore them. At first it makes you very bitter about them and the situation you're in, but gradually that goes away.

'The other thing is that you have to ignore what people say,' Will continued. 'We were a whole bunch of exhibitionists and most of what we said was rubbish – we were just looking for a reaction, and performing for a camera.' However, among those

9

:ople, he conceded, the lucky chosen few would form allegiances for life. 'It was a massive bonding experience and the people you get close to, you will carry on in your life for ever.'

Meanwhile, the next step was to choose one hundred candidates from the videos to present themselves for auditions and interviews in London. They, in turn, were whittled down, and some two months later twenty-eight eager contestants were invited to an adventure centre near Milton Keynes for the final selection weekend. Here, the group was really put through its paces – both physical, with outward bound-type activities, and mental, through in-depth interviews. For two days their leadership qualities and communication skills, not to mention their BIG personalities, were put to the test.

They had to undergo such initiative tests as trying to get around an obstacle course, in teams, on two planks of wood without their feet touching the ground. They did bungee runs. They needed to prove that they could build a barbecue and put up tents. The latter caused some extraordinary problems for a group of the girls and a young dancer named Stuart Bowden – eventually other, more tently-wise guys gave a hand. There was go-karting and water throwing and, as night drew in, the twenty-eight hopefuls began to look forward to some serious R&R. But how could anyone really relax with a camera crew on hand, and a television production team watching, judging and drawing conclusions?

In truth, the twenty-eight would-be shipwreckees had no problems in that department. It all began when Joanne Mills decided to throw a spanner in the works – or, more accurately, spin a bottle in a circle. The spinner had to snog whoever the bottle pointed at when it stopped, or pay the painful forfeit of standing over the campfire! Most people chose the kissing, and a wild snogathon ensued, with girls kissing girls, girls kissing boys

and boys kissing everyone. As Michael Lee, aka Blough, recalled later, 'It was like Ibiza gone mad, it was one of the great nights,' while Lucy Masaud declared in mock horror that 'the girls were rampant.' Samara Milford's verdict on the whole thing was that it was 'sordid'. Long after the camera had gone to bed, a bartender from Birmingham began a strip routine that quickly caught on with some of the late-nighters!

The following morning there was a mild post-mortem after the contestants were awakened rudely from their hangovers by the banging of saucepan lids before being frog-marched to the communal showers. Some could hardly see where they were going; others were willing to sell their soul, or anything else, for a cup of tea; to be frank, most of them had seen better days. Suddenly, someone realized that there were only twenty-seven contestants. One of their number was missing – Joanne. She who had started the revelries the night before by introducing spin-the-bottle; she who had shared a tent with two of the best-looking men in the camp – Tim Hitchens and Jody Chapman. And now, the following morning, she was gone. Neither of her tent-mates knew her whereabouts, claiming they had all gone to bed around two o'clock and at that point, Tim revealed, she was sharing a quilt with Jody. Now she had apparently disappeared into thin air.

But just as a rescue party was about to set out to find her, Joanne strolled into the camp, smiling and fully dressed, having spent the night in her car. 'I couldn't sleep in the tent, my back ached from the hard ground and my feet were cold,' she explained. 'In the end, I decided to spend the last few hours getting some decent sleep in my car.'

After breakfast, the applicants were set several more tests of strength and co-ordination, as well as undertaking more interviews with the production team. Now that each contestant

was more relaxed and their defences had started to come down a little, the questioning was more probing than before and the answers were more open. Asked what their worst habits were, some people responded with surprising – and occasionally unsavoury – replies. Vicky Oliver said she didn't like washing and didn't do it too often – when pushed by someone to confess to only having a bath once a week, she grinned and nodded. Tony Dunkels claimed his lavatorial habits were pretty hopeless, while Lucy said her worst trait was probably her tendency to mouth off at anything she didn't approve of, or like. In her defence, one of the production team observed that Lucy's bullshit detector was spot on.

In-between times, the girls discussed which of the men was the most fanciable. Tim and Jody got the vote. The duo had already been dubbed the Dream Team by the crew – they were the ones who got their tent up in less than five minutes and then set about helping everyone else. Lucy declared there were a couple of girls she fancied, but no way was she letting on who. Even the guys began to form friendships and bonds. Tim and Jody were not quite so close after their night with Joanne, and Jody became friendlier with Tony, whom the producers thought might be a bit 'posh' for the rest of the contestants – a comment shot down in flames by the accused. Kevin Thomas, a vision in bright pink shorts and vest, rather sweetly ventured that Tim not only had a great personality but was also too good-looking. A more vulnerable side of Kevin emerged as he told the producers during his interview about his upbringing, how he had been fostered, and how although his dad had taken him back for a while he was unable to keep him. Kev's throat caught as he explained that seeing his dad cry was the worst day of his life.

Victoria charmed everyone with her highly individual dress sense, incorporating multicoloured dreadlocks that adorned bits

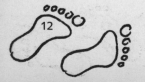

of her shaved head. She described herself as a 'little bit of a hippy with punk beliefs' and told the judges that she looked the way she did partly because it was different to everyone else in Wolverhampton, but also because it was conformist: when she was with her punk friends, they all dressed the same way! She impressed the judges with her openness and honesty. One judge commented that 'she talks straight from the heart, nothing is premeditated.'

Stuart, a gay dancer from Manchester, impressed everyone with the joy he seemed to take in virtually everything. From the minute he confessed he would have to take tweezers to the island with him – 'I just could not imagine appearing on camera with mismatching eyebrows' – he charmed the judges something rotten. In one of his more lengthy interviews with the production team and judges, he described his reactions to watching the first series. 'I was a great fan,' he admitted, 'but would sit there and criticize what they were doing, shouting at them and telling them what I would do under the same circumstances. I've dreamt about being shipwrecked and here I am,' and then with a great grin at the series producer, he added, 'I hope this whole trip will make a man out of me.' So, cheek and charm do work, and it was no surprise to anyone that the name of the first successful applicant to be announced was his. Interestingly, Stuart had already declared his enmity to the only other gay contestant – Lucy: 'She's already getting on my nerves; she's too mouthy'.

While the co-ordination and speed tests carried on outside, the interviews continued in the main huts. Blough explained that although he had trained as a chef, music was his great love and his life: 'It is what I do twenty-four hours a day – I write, rap and listen. I have no money. I'm on the dole, but I give all of that to my mum for the housekeeping; nothing means that much to me except my music.' On a lighter note, Jody talked about what it was like living with a girl's name for twenty years and Andrew

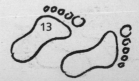

Douglas explained what a huge part football played in his life – 'it is what I had always wanted' – and how turning professional was the highlight of his life so far. As he left the interview, one of the producers pointed out that half of the female viewing population would fall in love with Andy before the series had reached its halfway point, and he was dubbed 'The Smile that Launched a Thousand Heartbreaks'.

Joanne, on the other hand, explained that she was really looking forward to living without make-up and confessed the worst thing about being considered pretty was that you were constantly judged by your looks. Challenged by the judges that if she were chosen she might think it would be for her looks alone, her reply was careful and sensitive. While acknowledging that looks (and make no mistake, we're dealing with a *Baywatch* babe-type here) obviously play a part, Jo said she hoped that if she were chosen, it would be for more than her appearance.

However, many of them were distinctly economical with the truth. When the final fourteen were chosen, it transpired that all but four of them were in a relationship – a fact they had omitted to reveal during the selection process. What this meant in the end was that they were all very careful about their behaviour on camera, so as not to upset the partners they had left behind – thus discouraging any hopes of serious nookie on Nuku. However, as everyone soon discovered, there are many ways of behaving badly when you are away from home…

Meanwhile, on the other side of the world another group of hopefuls were being put through their paces in New South Wales, Australia. For the twist in the sails of *Shipwrecked* series two was that the British fourteen were going to be joined by three Australians in a bi-cultural exercise. The first series had gone down a storm in Australia, and when the call went out looking for volunteers to join another run of *Shipwrecked*, more

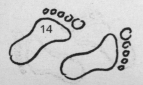

than 10,000 applied for the show. Again, the thousands had to be whittled down to a handful for the final selection weekend. At a naval training centre on the outskirts of Sydney, ten hopefuls turned up to battle it out for the three available places. The Australian physical tests were much more rigorous than their English equivalents, and had two teams of five battling through blood, sweat and tears to be chosen. Their physical toughness was tested to the limit – co-ordination, speed and strength were pushed to the max time and time again over two days. The applicants had to swing on ropes and walk across logs; wearing harnesses and helmets, they climbed and abseiled.

Lisa Kastaniotis faced a real test of character when the group was asked to climb fifty feet up a tree and then cross to another tree on a rope bridge suspended with wires. Fine, if you like that sort of a thing and are a hairy-kneed, outward-bound sort of cove, but if you are a five-foot-nothing female terrified of heights, the situation becomes seriously traumatic. Lisa confessed to her team that she was scared of heights and was given dispensation to stand down or drop out from the task. 'But you can't really do that,' she admitted. 'I've always thought that you have to go for it – but I have to say it was the most terrifying thing I have ever done. Getting onto that ladder I was too frightened to keep my eyes open or to look down – the first rung was the worst.' However, given huge encouragement from her team, she slowly worked her away across the treacherous bridge; as she got to the final step, she collapsed in tears of relief. The final test was known as the 'Spider's Web' – an intricate lattice of rope that each contestant had to pass through without touching it with any part of their body or clothing. The daring ones simply propelled themselves straight through it, launching themselves onto the ground a few feet away. The exhibitionists removed much of their clothing before starting out, while the attention seekers were

man-handled through by the rest of the team. One team managed the whole contest in just four minutes, while the second team took more than five times as long.

Eventually, three individuals emerged to defend the honour of Oz on that little Pacific island. And, of course, one of those three was the plucky and vociferous Lisa. The other two were Dharma Bendersky (known to his friends as D) an all-out, typical Australian action man, and Larissa Walker, a pretty blonde. Larissa is a former model and frankly admitted that she loves being in front of a camera.

Meanwhile, back in Milton Keynes, tension was mounting. The forty-eight hours of tests and trials were almost up, and soon half of the contestants would be sent home with just the memories of a fun weekend, while the others would have the promise of one of the greatest experiences of their life to look forward to. They waited... and waited. The judges were locked in debate; while eight contestants sailed through, there was much to discuss about the remaining six. The series needed balance as well as performance, characters as well as exhibitionists. Two hours passed and the pressure began to show in some of the faces. A desultory game of football took place in one area; whispered conversations and nervous laughter was heard in another. Eventually, the door opened and out stepped the judges to explain that the names of the fourteen successful applicants were about to be called out. They were at pains to point out how difficult the choice had been – much more so than for the first series, they admitted – and that it was a magnificent achievement for all of the applicants to have made it through from the initial 20,000.

Then, silence... Everybody looked straight ahead and tried to appear nonchalant. The announcement of the first name – Stuart – brought a round of applause for him and simple relief for everybody else. The countdown had started. And then, in

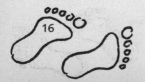

quick succession, the other names were called out and each lucky applicant stood and moved down to one side of the deck to gather with the other lucky winners. The names were Victoria Oliver, Michael 'Blough' Lee, Lucy Masaud, Tony Dunkels, Beth Golding, Jody Chapman, Joanne Mills, Andrew Douglas, Emma-Rosa Dias, Tim Hitchens, Samara Milford, Lucy Taylor and Kevin Thomas. Relief and euphoria combined on the faces of fourteen of the happiest, most excited people in the UK that day. Kev wiped away a tear as he hugged his new friends, while Stuart wept openly.

The weekend was over, but the adventure was about to begin. For in less than six weeks, these fourteen relative strangers would travel halfway around the world and attempt to cope not only with each other, but also with circumstances that were as alien to them as if they had been sent to Mars. Their lives would never be quite the same again. In fact, by the time they left England, they were already mini-celebrities – they were photographed for magazines, interviewed by newspapers and had appeared on television. They had been made up for cameras and styled for photographs – their fifteen minutes of fame was well and truly under way. But would it all be worth it?

The island of Nuku, with its sun-kissed beaches – considered to be the best in Tonga – and tropical vegetation, covers about eight acres in total. It was chosen mainly for its location, which is far enough away from the mainland to seem remote but close enough in case of emergency. Its nearest neighbour is the island of Fukave, about a kilometre away – this too was completely deserted, apart from the occasional fisherman. Each member of the *Shipwrecked* cast was told they could spend one night on that island with the person of their choice without any members of crew or camera following them… It became one of the great guessing games to see who would go with whom, and when.

17

The nearest inhabited island was just five kilometres away, and housed Tonga's high-security prison. This novel piece of information later gave rise to the lads' attempt to scare the girls with tales of voices in the night, missing machetes and escaped convicts. Things came to a head when a T-shirt belonging to a cast member was found washed up on Fukave. The whole episode caused many sleepless nights and a general fear of going to the long-drop (the lavatory) alone at night!

But Nuku itself, apart from the mosquitoes, was more or less paradise. It was surrounded by two reefs – one a barrier reef, and the other less dense, with a small opening allowing boats access to the shore. The reefs were home to the most amazing collection of fish and coral as well as a number of passing sharks, which added a certain frisson to the daily fishing expeditions. In fact, when the first shark was spotted by Kev, Jody and Tony, all they could do was marvel at its beauty; Kev swimming after it to see it more clearly. All three agreed it was one of the most amazing things they had ever seen, and once they brought the fish they had caught in, they went straight back out to see if they could find it again.

Three months before the cast arrived on the island, half an acre was cleared in the centre, which was then planted with a number of vegetables for their use – cabbage, lettuce, sweet potato, squash, arrowroot and tomatoes – all of which was ready by their first week on Nuku. And, by a great stroke of good luck, the crew found an abandoned canoe on one of the beaches, left by a local fisherman. They roughed it up a little, so that the cast had to fix and mend it before taking it off to the mainland for rations and relaxation. All the essential supplies that might be needed by the seventeen cast members were taken to Nuku beforehand and hidden around the place for them to find. These included lamps, tarpaulins, matches, lamps, fuel, mosquito nets,

cooking equipment, fishing nets and gardening tools, along with some rope, food and nails. In fact, most of the things necessary to make their new-found paradise habitable – all the cast had to do was uncover them.

But first, the mixed bag of the cast – which included an advertising student, a lawyer, a professional footballer, a punk, a designer and a dancer – had to be taught survival techniques. Five days' acclimatization was allowed on the mainland before they were taken to the island. Their appointed tutor was a local called Ernie – whom one cast member later described as her South Pacific grandfather – helped by his son, Norris. Ernie was to be the cast's link to the mainland throughout their time on Nuku, bringing their weekly rations and luxuries.

And, of course, they had to meet their Australian co-habitees, turning up at Tonga's main airport to welcome them half a day after the Brit contingent had arrived from the other side of the world. There was a good-natured atmosphere, and all seventeen were full of great expectations – this was, after all, as they kept saying, the chance of a lifetime. Everyone was determined to like each other, to have a great time and to make the great adventure work for both themselves and the television series. But would it?

The cast spent this precious preparatory time learning to fish and manage a boat on Pangaimotu, a tiny nearby island. In-between times, they began to get to know each other, chilling out in the sunshine, feeling their first pangs of homesickness, forming new alliances, engaging in gentle flirtations, getting drunk… and waiting. When the day eventually arrived for the group to leave civilization as they knew it and depart for their deserted isle, nature stepped in and brought a tropical storm, which put them on tenterhooks for yet another day…

Was this an omen?

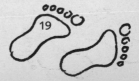

CONTRACT

Dear

Re: "Shipwrecked" ("the Project")

Firstly, my congratulations again on being selected to participate in the Shipwrecked Project.

I am writing now to confirm the terms on which we agree to allow you to, and you consent to, participate in the Project. Please read your obligations set out below carefully and note that breaching any of these obligations may result in you being removed from participation in the Project.

A. In consideration of us arranging to film and record the contribution to be given by you to us in respect of the Project YOU AGREE:

 1. that you have had explained to you, and fully understand, the nature and risks of the Project and your participation in it and you agree to so participate;

 2. that we will only allow you to withdraw from participation in the Project in exceptional circumstances (for example severe illness or family bereavement);

 3. that you will at all times promptly and faithfully comply with all instructions of our representatives (and you understand that this is not only to facilitate filming, but at times may be in the interests of your or other's safety);

 4. that at no time will you engage in behaviour which endangers the successful completion of the Project or the safety of yourself or others;

5. that you will adhere to the system of 'laws', decision-making procedures and democracy governing your time on the island, which will be provided to you before you leave;

6. that you will not, without our prior consent or at our request, make to any third party any statement or supply any information or photograph relating to the Project or to the terms hereof. Nor will you contact or attempt to contact any of the other participants in the Project prior to your departure for the island;

7. that you will not, without our prior consent, voluntarily engage in any hazardous pursuit nor take any risk the taking of which would invalidate or affect any normal policy of insurance on your life or health effected in connection with the Project or might interfere with your participation in the Project;

8. that you are not now nor have at any time been subject to or suffering from any injury, ailment, incapacity, condition, indisposition or the like which might adversely affect your ability or suitability to participate in the Project;

9. to the recording (at any and all times as we may elect) and broadcasting of your contribution to the Project and hereby give all consents necessary for the reproduction, exhibition, transmission, broadcast, publicising, previewing, reviewing and exploitation of your contribution without time limit throughout the universe by all means and

media (whether now known or hereafter discovered or developed) without liability or acknowledgement to you;

10. *that your contribution will be true and honest and that we shall be entitled to cut, edit or translate your contribution as we deem fit and we shall not be obliged to include all or any of your contribution in any programme.*

11. *that you have disclosed to us full and complete details of any and all criminal convictions that you have.*

B. *You also acknowledge that we have, and will continue throughout the Project to take all reasonable measures to ensure your safety, but you recognise that there are risks inherent in the nature of the Project and you agree that we shall not be liable to you in the event of any personal injury or ailment or death arising out of or in the course of your participation in the Project except to such extent, if at all, as the same was due to our negligence.*

C. *You further agree that:*

In the event that you write any diaries, articles, books or other written works during your stay on the island or subsequently and which are based in the main on your experiences at the island ("the Written Works"), you agree that during the period commencing on the date hereof and continuing until the later date of one year from the date of this Agreement or six months from the delivery of the Written Works to Channel 4:

1. you will not disclose to any third party the contents of the Written Works or any part thereof or any details thereof;

2. you will not enter into or pursue any negotiations with any third party relating to the publication or exploitation rights in or to the Written Works,

and;

3. you will not give any commitment to any third party to grant, or to enter into or pursue any negotiations relating to any publication or exploitation rights in the Written Works.

You will provide a copy of the Written Works to Channel 4 within 28 days of leaving the island, or, if written after leaving the island, within 28 days of writing such Written Works. Channel 4 will advise you within two months whether it wishes to publish or otherwise exploit the Written Works, you agree to negotiate in good faith and with reasonable expedition the terms on which we may do so and you agree that you will co-operate and consult with any person involved in the writing of any book about the Project and/or any publishing or exploitation of the Written Works.

Please ensure that you have read and fully understand the above obligations before you sign this letter.

KIT LIST

Dear

The big day is fast approaching and, in order for you to prepare yourself in time, we are enclosing a list of items that you need to think about bringing to the island, a document outlining health and safety issues, and the island rules (as referred to in your contracts). You'll also find enclosed another copy of the contract and details of the insurance cover for your own records.

Whilst you don't have to bring all the items on the kit list we are insisting that everyone brings a hat, sunglasses, lightweight waterproof jacket and at least two warm jumpers or fleeces. We also require you to bring your own sleeping bag.

Everything that you pack must fit in the bag we provide, the only exceptions being sleeping bags and any larger luxury items approved by the production team. We will provide plenty of shampoo, soap, moisturizing lotion, mosquito repellents and nets, and medical supplies (including vitamins, tampons and condoms but not toilet paper). Any other toiletries, excluding personal medication, hairbrushes, toothbrushes, toothpaste, tweezers and razors, will be counted as luxury items. A doctor will regularly visit the island to ensure your well-being and it is vital that you inform us of any personal medication (asthma inhalers, birth control pills etc) as soon as possible.

As you're all aware, we allow everyone to bring three luxury items with them, and we would encourage you to think of things that might be of practical use or good for entertainment. You cannot bring anything that is battery operated, clockwork radios, watches, telescopes/ binoculars or cameras. We will be checking all bags before we depart so if you are in any doubt please ask beforehand, otherwise you may lose a luxury.

Anyone who would like to bring a notebook or diary as a luxury item may do so on the understanding that they may occasionally be asked to pick out and read excerpts to the camera.

You may bring alcohol provided it fits into your bag and does not exceed the Customs limit (1 litre of spirits and 2 litres of still table wine). But those of you wishing to bring tobacco and rolling papers must include them as one of your luxury items and keep within Customs limits (250g). Filter tipped cigarettes will not be permitted.

RDF Productions will obviously meet the costs for all accommodation, food and medical requirements, but you will be spending three days on the mainland undergoing survival training and may want to bring a small amount of spending money for extra drinks, souvenirs and phone calls home. If you complete the full duration on the island you will also be offered the opportunity to delay your flight home, so should come financially prepared for this if you think it is something you are likely to do.

Finally, it goes without saying that anyone discovered bringing drugs, weapons (excluding penknives, leather-men etc) or anything else illegal will be sent home IMMEDIATELY or end up languishing in a Tongan jail where, it's worth noting, they still have the death penalty! Sorry if this all sounds rather finicky, but I think you'll agree that it will all be worth it in the end! If you have any queries please give us a call.

Good luck!

Shipwreckee's Own Kit

We have provided you with a bag which is just small enough to be taken as hand luggage and we suggest you bring the following items ...

Hat (this is obligatory)
Sunglasses (these are obligatory)
Normal glasses if required/contact lenses if you prefer

Shorts (max 3 prs)
Sarongs (max 3)
Swimwear (max 3)
Long cotton trousers (max 2)
Warm long trousers (1 pr)
Long sleeved cotton shirt (max 2)
T shirts/vest tops etc (max 4)
Socks (max 2 prs)
Underwear (max 4 sets)
Sandals/flip-flops (1 pr)
Trainers (1 pr)
Lightweight waterproof jacket (1)
3 Warm sweaters or fleeces (these are obligatory)
Toothbrush, toothpaste, comb/hairbrush and razor.
All other toiletries (eg shampoo, sun cream,

moisturiser) will be supplied by us. Sleeping bag
(Don't rush out and buy anything posh – you can
always get army surplus if you can't swipe one from
home.)
3 luxury items which must be approved by
the production – (nothing battery operated,
no watches, no clock-work radios, no telescopes/
binoculars or cameras – try and think of things
which will be of practical use or good for
entertainment)

Any personal medication (such as asthma inhalers,
birth control pills etc. Please advise us of what
this is)
Painkillers (such as paracetamol or aspirin).
Health and Safety regulations prevent us from
distributing painkillers, so you may want to bring a
small personal supply.

**Everything you take, except the sleeping bag and
things like guitars, must fit in the bag we give you.**

CONSTITUTION

1. Once a week, the group will hold a meeting which all seventeen contributors MUST attend.

   The first meeting will take place on the day of arrival on the island, before dark. The second meeting will take place two or three days later on a day to be specified by the production, and then weekly from then on. The group is free to hold additional meetings as and when they desire.

2. At the weekly meeting, the group will elect, or re-elect, a leader for the following week. The group will vote for two candidates before making its final choice by a secret ballot. One person, one vote, and the winner is the person with the most votes. In the case of a draw, the two tied candidates will draw lots.

3. The previously elected leader will act as chairman at these meetings, and must ensure that everybody gets their chance to speak, each in turn and not all at once!

4. Each member of the group is bound to follow the leader's decisions. If, at any point during the week, they are unwilling to do so, then the matter will be put to the rest of the group and their decision will be binding.

5. In recognition of the work and responsibilities of leadership, the leader will have the privilege of his/her own 'luxury' bed, provided by us, which he/she must use themselves.

6. The group will be given two cameras with which to film themselves. One of these cameras will be secured in a secluded area away from the camp to provide complete privacy. Each member of the group must visit this camera at least once a week to record some of their thoughts. It is fundamental that members of the group respect each other's privacy whilst using this facility. The camera will be fixed in such a way that no one will be able to view another person's footage or record over it. The group will be trained how to use the second camera themselves, and anyone in the group is allowed to use it to shoot anything they want during the ten weeks, on the understanding that the material shot belongs to the production and may well be used in the final programmes.

7. Each member of the group will be allowed to spend one night on the neighbouring island. It is up to them to decide when and with whom they go, but they can only use this privilege once. For safety reasons, a member of the crew must accompany them, but they will not be filmed and the crew member will allow them complete privacy by camping at a reasonable distance.

8. Voluntarily leaving the island: should someone wish to leave the island themselves or think that another member of the group should leave on compassionate grounds, they may put this to the vote at a group meeting. There must be at least fourteen votes for the

motion. The only compassionate grounds on which an individual can put themselves or someone else forward to be voted off the island are medical/health problems, bad news from back home (which will be relayed by the production) or mental distress. In any case, they must seek the permission of the production to put themselves or someone else forward for such a vote (such permission not to be unreasonably withheld, but boredom does not equal 'mental distress'!).

9. Compulsory expulsion from the island: If an individual or individuals want to propose the expulsion of another member of the group they may approach the leader in confidence. The leader will then be obliged to present the proposal to the group at the weekly meeting. The individual in question must be given an opportunity to defend himself/ herself before the rest of the group vote on the final decision. The voting will be done by secret ballot and there must be at least fourteen votes in favour for the expulsion to be carried out.

10. If anyone is expelled or chooses to leave the island before the end of the project, they will be put on the first available flight back to the UK. Those that stay to the end of the period may be able to delay their return flight to the UK, should they so wish.

11. The group will be given a master list of rations. This list will detail the entire quantity of food which will

be available to the group to supplement what can be gleaned from the island. Each week, the leader must place an order for rations which will then be delivered the following week and deducted from the master list.

12. The group will also be given a choice of 'luxury items' for which they can vote once a week. The item that gets the most votes will be delivered with the weekly rations.

13. Apart from the above, the group may vote additional island 'laws' as they desire, by simple majority, but these must be ratified by the production (approval not to be unreasonably withheld).

14. The producer has absolute discretion to remove any individual whose behaviour, for any reason, is deemed to threaten the success of this enterprise.

THE CASTAWAYS

Dharma Bendersky

Stuart Bowden

Jody Chapman

Emma-Rosa Dias

Andrew Douglas

Anthony Dunkels

Beth Golding

Tim Hitchens

Lisa Kastaniotis

Michael Lee

Lucy Masaud

Samara Milford

Joanne Mills

Victoria Oliver

Lucy Taylor

Kevin Thomas

Larissa Walker

A real outdoor Aussie action man, D, as he liked to be called, was playing the Aussie-versus-Poms angle before he even got to the island. He thought the group from the first series was a bunch of whingers that sat around doing nothing all day. Indeed, for a long time D thought some of the cast of *Shipwrecked* series two were similarly inclined, although he was complimentary about Tony, whom he thought was absolutely the best person to be the first leader because he was positive and led by example. D was the first cast member to explore the island and found supplies of rice and rum as well as the garden. However, although he was mentioned frequently as having the potential to be a good leader, he was never nominated. This frustrated him so much that at one stage he was about to ask the Aussie girls to nominate him, simply to see how many votes he would get.

D was seriously upset at not being chosen for either of the ration runs, although he was the most obvious person for the task. When the re-votes were about to take place for the first time in public, he vented his spleen, castigating the rest of them for neither nominating nor voting for him. However, that approach did not work either, and it was only Tim's act of supreme generosity that got him off the island. D was stunned and greatly moved by this gesture. It seemed that there was such a thing as a good Pom after all!

D felt isolated almost from the very beginning – firstly by being the only Aussie male, and secondly by his own attitude and expectations for the stay on the island. He came to test his

33

survival instincts and to learn about himself, but claimed most of the Brits 'don't want to learn. They're not interested in living here – they just want to get a tan.' However, he did admit that the Aussies had much more outdoor experience than the Brits. He joined in everything and was determined that although he had little in common with the group he would still try to interact. But he found it more and more difficult to involve himself in talks and chats – he didn't understand the British sense of humour and thought he would go crazy in the first few weeks if he heard any more jokes about farting.

He got on best with the other two Aussies and Lucy M: 'people see her as different and I suppose we are different too, which is why we clicked.' In the early stages he was already looking for a place of his own, and once he found it he planned to build a shelter and move there. But not before he had set up and organized the island Olympics, to mirror the real games taking place in Sydney at the same time. Not surprisingly, his team – which consisted of himself, Tim, Jo and Lucy M – won.

What D didn't realize was that a lot of the cast admired him. It wasn't really until the last two weeks that he seriously began interacting with everybody and getting on with them.

Name: *Stuart Bowden*
From: **Manchester**   Age: **20**
Luxuries: hammock, tobacco, the book *Sophie's World*

Fun, flamboyant and very camp, Stuart is of mixed race, gay and a professional dancer, having just completed his degree in Dance. An only child who is extremely proud of his working-class roots, he admits that he has never gone without anything. The only time he upset his parents was when he admitted his sexuality. He says his father was fine about it and very accepting, but his mother was quite the opposite. However, when he split up from his boyfriend and went home heartbroken to Mum, all differences were resolved.

Stuart's interests include photography, philosophy, theatre, fashion and gymnastics, and the latter must have helped turn him into the champion coconut tree climber on the island. He was extremely popular, both at the selection weekend and with the rest of the cast on the island. At first Kevin admitted that he was a bit of a homophobe and had never really mixed with gays, but within days he was a great admirer of Stuart. For his part, Andy felt that Stu was a 'fantastic ambassador for the gay community'. Stuart was both thrilled and touched to be voted leader: 'The respect and admiration I've been getting from the group is overwhelming. I've always been liked, but this is respect.'

And yet, in spite of all of this, he was occasionally overwhelmed by loneliness and homesickness. 'It's fine during the day when there are lots of things to do, but at night it is really, really lonely. But I came here to get to know myself, and the biggest challenge is for me to accept this loneliness. I have been lonely before – I'm an only child – but I don't think that I will be this lonely again, ever.'

Stuart had one of the most difficult tasks to cope with during his leadership, when a re-vote was demanded for the ration run, as two of the lads had 'betrayed the trust' of the others by stealing the last of the rum. There was a lot of hurt and anger in the camp, and Stuart had to deal with it. 'It was the biggest drama of my leadership – I had to make the decisions, and it was a good experience. I got annoyed by some people's attitude to meetings, but we're developing a democracy here and when you accept something like this you have to compromise.'

Stuart was quick to notice the changing nature of the atmosphere on the island and spotted that it was around the fifth week

when the real textures and colours of people's personalities were coming out. But right at the very beginning, his shrewdness and understanding came to the fore over Lucy M's determination to put up her rainbow flag: 'If it makes her feel better that's OK. But I really don't want a big flag in my face reminding me how different I am from everyone, because I don't see it as a difference, and flags have always been known to separate people.'

Although he got on with both the boys and the girls, Stuart spent most of the time with the girls – particularly Lisa, with whom he formed a strong bond. She invited him to come and stay with her in Australia and he wants her to come visit him in England.

Name: *Jody Chapman*
From: **Dorset**   Age: **23**
Luxuries: chess set, book, sketch book

Jody was nominated by his sister for *Shipwrecked*. She commented: 'He is an impossibly nice guy, can always be relied on in a crisis, is a wonderful brother and uncle and is still loved by all his ex-girlfriends.' A design graduate, Jody is returning to a job in car interior design. He is mad about music and mountain biking and spent his gap year in the States working as a mechanic for a drag-racing team. Jody says he likes designing things and cooking and is good at creating solutions. He was very popular at the selection weekend – particularly with the girls – and says he has no problems in building relationships.

Jody claims he was genuinely surprised to be picked and was delighted to be chosen, although he was worried about making the final selection weekend in case it clashed with his degree show, which would have to take priority. Fortunately, it was

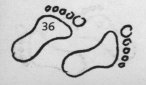

exactly a week later. He regarded the chance to be shipwrecked as a once-in-a-lifetime opportunity: 'I wouldn't be able to do this at any time in my life but now. It was college before and work after, so there would never have been the time for ten weeks on a desert island.'

He was elected leader in the second week, which really thrilled him, although he was worried that he wouldn't be able to keep up all the good work done by Tony, who did the job first. 'I get on well with Tony, more than any of the others, and I know I can rely on him to help me with my duties.' The two guys really bonded. Tony paid tribute to all the help he had been given by Jody in the first week and knows that everybody had a lot of respect for Jody – apart from Lucy M, who described him as 'Tony's little henchman'.

Quiet and good-looking, Jody got on really well with Larissa (he says she's cute) and often the two were found together on the beach or in the hammock, although he also claimed to be missing his ex-girlfriend a lot.

Jody is quite sensitive and he worried about his leadership and whether he was showing the right qualities – he didn't feel he was strong enough at motivating people and often ended up doing things himself rather than delegating, although Jo pointed out later it was management, not delegation, that was needed. And he was also very distressed about the problems between Lucy M and Tony: 'Tony tried to make things better with her, but she just took no notice. The whole situation had a very bad effect on morale. I hate confrontations and would do anything to avoid them.'

Even though the group seem to get on well enough, Jody found it hardest to deal with the lack of privacy and the lack of intelligent conversation, 'The rain made it worse, because you have seventeen people in a completely confined space all trying

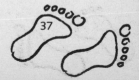

to out-talk each other.' Larissa told Jody that he was the quietest member of the group, which made him worry that he was considered an outsider or a recluse. 'I just need my own personal space,' he maintained. Jody realizes that people see him as thoughtful and intelligent, and he dubs himself 'the quiet intellectual'.

Name: *Emma-Rosa Digs*
From: **Belfast**   Age: **24**
Luxuries: diary, yoga book, box of spices

This Afro-Irish castaway admits to being very competitive and a flirt while at the same time describing herself as both sexy and super-sensitive. She feels her job as a nightclub promoter is extremely stressful, which is why a sojourn on an abandoned island may have been just the break she needed. However, she also works in an Internet cafe and as an aerobics instructor and is a great enthusiast for both yoga and aromatherapy. A self-confessed health freak, she doesn't eat foods that contain white flour or sugar and never touches red meat.

During the selection process Emma-Rosa was disliked by many of the other girls, who thought she was aloof and condescending. This was compounded when she did not get involved in the snogging and various other shenanigans on the Saturday night – preferring to sit quietly chatting and observing. Some members of the cast felt that she seemed arrogant and appeared to think herself too mature for the kinds of activities the others were enjoying, and this continued on the island – as Emma-Rosa herself said, 'It's like a real-life soap opera here.' However, for most of that weekend she was inseparable from

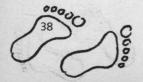

Stuart Bowden, and their friendship continued to grow and strengthen on the island. Her other main friendships were with Samara and Jo.

Like many of the shipwreckers, she left a boyfriend at home and declared that what she will miss most, in no particular order, are: boyfriend, mother, *EastEnders* and chips.

Emma-Rosa became one of the main cooks on the island, although she occasionally upset the others by being bossy about the food and rations. The most frequent complaint against her was that she never said please or thank you, although her worst moment came when she was forced to admit to stealing cans of mackerel.

One of her main aims in coming to the island was to get really fit. She gave up smoking before getting there and taught Jo aerobics; the two of them worked out on the beach together every morning.

Name: *Andrew Douglas*
From: **Hertfordshire**   Age: **20**
Luxuries: book, diary, football

A Jamaican professional footballer, Andy was considered the best-looking boy on the island. He's a real charmer and not as laddish as he might initially appear – indeed, he was one of the first to step back when things began to get slightly out of hand at the selection weekend. He had just completed his second season with Sheffield Wednesday FC when he was chosen for *Shipwrecked* – but was then devastated to learn that his contract wasn't being renewed. Prior to Sheffield he had had a two-year apprenticeship with Arsenal, and although he's been offered

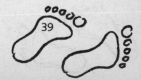

places with a couple of lower-division clubs, he's not sure what he is going to do next.

Andrew's older brother is doing well playing for Luton, so Andy continued training with him until he left for the island and decided to make a decision about his footballing future on his return. 'I had only ever been interested in football until I made the decision to come here. I know that there is more to life, but that's all I ever wanted. Now I have decided that I've given ten years of my life to the game, so for ten weeks I'm going to concentrate on me.'

He was thrilled to be chosen as leader in the fourth week: 'I was one of the youngest and yet people trusted me with the role. It's a real privilege and shows they must have respect for me.' Yet he was delighted to give the job up at the end of his term: 'you never have a moment to relax, because people are asking you stuff the whole time!' But more than anything he was thrilled to be chosen as one of the four guys to do the ration run – he and Kev were voted in as the second team – and was more than 'gutted' when they were thought to have blown their opportunity by stealing rum. The looks on both of their faces during the discussion and re-vote showed despair and disbelief.

Andrew's a clever guy, with a good number of GCSEs and a distinction in a Leisure and Tourism GNVQ. He is shrewd in his summing up of people and situations. Although he took against the rainbow flag to begin with, believing that among seventeen individuals certain issues should be left at home, he ended up having great admiration for Lucy M and the way she defended herself in the stealing row. He liked her toughness and conviction. He also understood Vic's alienation: 'she has no direction and it dawned on her only when she got here, which is why she feels really lost and isolated.' And he was one of the first to realize that this paradise meant more than just sunshine and blue seas – it also meant 'soggy rice and other people'. He admitted that it had taken five weeks for him to realize how alone he was: 'I'm not sure I have one true friend here – I thought I was everyone's mate when they voted me for leader'.

Name: *Anthony Dunkels*
From: **London**   Age: **23**
Luxuries: guitar, hammock, fishing stuff

The archetypal posh public schoolboy. Harrow-educated, Tony got A grades and distinctions in everything and is now doing a CPE course at the College of Law in London, where he has been elected as staff-student representative. A political animal and a shrewd observer, he had all the markings of being *Shipwrecked*'s answer to Nasty Nick. During the team-building exercises he was constantly volunteering himself as group leader – an offer that was not taken up by the group. However, they elected him as leader the minute they got on the island, feeling that his confidence and capabilities were ideal to get them started in their new home. In fact, some of them would have been quite happy for him to remain as leader throughout. Tony was fairly pleased with the way the week developed, commenting that he was quite proud of the group and the way they had worked, although he wished that a few had shown more initiative. However, he doubted whether anyone else could have done a better job of leadership.

Tony was tireless in getting the shelter built and the long-drop dug and was also one of the most frequent fishermen. He

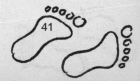

felt that if people saw him working, they would follow suit. Alas, this was not to be so in every case.

Tony was one of the few members of the cast who has lived in another country – he spent nine months working on a conservation project in Australia and has also travelled extensively and independently in northern China, Nepal, India, Africa and Tibet. And while he was at university he organized rallies and meetings for the Free Tibet society. His other interests include playing the guitar, Latin American dance, mountain biking and herpetology – he has eleven snakes. Attractive and a tad arrogant, he has a number of large tattoos on his chest and arms.

Tony struck up an instant and strong friendship with Jody – he even snogged him on the selection weekend – and most of the boys got on with him, even if they didn't become close friends. He was one of the few Poms that Australian D both liked and admired. In fact, most of the girls also liked him, although Lucy M certainly did not. It was the antagonism between them that provided one of the first and most bitter confrontations. She thought him a misogynist and a sexist pig who had one face for the camera and another for the rest of them, while he thought her a 'highly intelligent, manipulative, evil human being.' When Lucy apologized to him over labelling him a sexist, he claims he did not want to accept the apology because he knew it was not genuine. But not accepting it would have thrown the group into turmoil. He even thought about leaving, but was told by Jody and others that if he did, Lucy would have effectively won. Lucy's only rebuttal was that she would think it an insult to be liked or accepted by somebody like Tony.

A country girl working as a PA in London, Beth is straightforward and down to earth. In fact, she was nominated the person most deserving of being picked by the rest of the contributors. She has boyish good looks and a few tattoos and claims to be actively looking for a boyfriend but, because she thinks most of the men she meets in London are rude and immature, feels she may be fighting a losing battle. Her hobbies are food, drink, rollerblading and roller coasters. Despite her youth, Beth came across as one of the more mature members of the group.

She did not join in the snogging shenanigans at the selection weekend and thinks that everyone else apart from her is looking for sex. She is very fair-minded and became cross when people were being selfish and not considering the group. She felt that people got on quite well, although there were occasional differences of opinion. Beth herself didn't see the point of arguing; her view was that people should be aware of each other's differences and at least be polite to each other. She felt that the island was too beautiful a place to argue in: 'Surely we can all shut up for ten weeks? It is almost like paradise, why won't they stop arguing?'

Beth is quick to spot other people's Achilles' heels and has a strong sense of fair play – for instance, she became very distressed when someone broke her badminton racquet and didn't own up to it, and got really cross when she discovered that Lucy M had been stealing food from the crew camp – so much so that she felt obliged to confront her. She brought that same

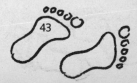

43

straightforwardness to bear on D. Beth realized that he was having difficulty bonding with the group, but felt he should show more consideration for others – she cited the way he snapped at the girls and his lack of concern over whether there was milk or fresh water for coffee in the mornings, provided he got his.

Beth applauded Tony for recognizing that Lucy M didn't like him and for skirting around that problem. She got on very well with Lucy T, whom she described as being loud and clever. She found Tim very attractive and got on really well with him – though only as a friend – and was great friends with Stuart. She was also one of the few people on the island that Kevin confided in, telling her all about his home life and showing her pictures of his family. Beth realized very early on that the girls were much more divided than the boys and that it was probably caused by jealousy over looks, which is why she felt it easier to bond with the boys to begin with. And she shrewdly pointed out the difference in attitude to their sexuality between Lucy M and Stuart. Beth felt that Lucy was proud of making a statement about her gayness while Stuart was simply getting on with it.

Although she was prone to don her fairy wings for the confessional camera, Beth's views and opinions were both pragmatic and understanding of other people's shortcomings and foibles. She confessed very early on that she would like to be leader but had no idea how the group rated her, especially as she felt she was 'rubbish at telling people what to do'. However, many of the boys thought she would make a very good leader, and proposed her.

Beth was one of the few girls to attempt to kill the chickens and also to help pluck and gut them. She was also the group's gardener and looked after their vegetable patch with devotion.

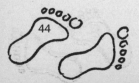

Name: *Tim Hitchens*
From: **London**   Age: **23**
Luxuries: sketch book, hammock, frisbee

Confident, good-looking and gregarious, Tim claims to make the best of every situation and to get on with people – although during the selection weekend he came across as cocky and arrogant: people thought he was loud and too 'up himself'. However, on the island he was liked by almost everyone. He worked hard, was fun to be with and performed the only truly noble act of the entire ten weeks when he gave up his place on the ration run to D.

Just before being selected for *Shipwrecked*, Tim was high-lighted in the *Daily Telegraph* as being one of Britain's sharpest design talents. Having worked for the Conran Group after university, it didn't take him long to realize he would be better off using his own voice and working on his own – which is when he set up a small workshop, from which he now operates.

Tim has a long-term girlfriend – they have known each other since school – and apparently she was not too happy about him being away for so long. He, on the other hand, was really looking forward to the break and formed a number of friendships with both the lads and the girls. On the selection weekend he was very taken with Jo, whom he snogged, and spent most of the night with, before she moved out to her car.

On the island he developed a real friendship with both Beth and Stuart and in fact the three of them spent twenty-four hours in Los Angeles together before returning home. And according to a quick poll amongst the girls, Tim came first in the 'if you had to sleep with one of them who would it be' stakes. He joined

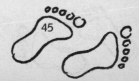

in with the lads – Blough, Kev and Andy – in their 'let's scare the girls' exercise, but each evening he would walk around the island with Beth and discuss their worries, hopes and loneliness.

Occasionally Tim questioned the whole exercise: 'I thought I would learn something different about myself – but so far I haven't – except back home I am really protective about my possessions, but I haven't missed any of them.' He said part of his reason for going to the island was to become a 'different, stronger person – maybe I will when I get back.'

About halfway through, Tim developed what he termed a 'deep craving' for decent conversation. He felt there was no intellectual stimulation on the island and couldn't believe what most people talked about – sex and food – non-stop. He thought it was a great advantage to see the first series: 'they were the real guinea pigs; we are guinea pigs with jackets on.'

He was voted leader in the sixth week and loved the task. Although it was during his leadership that the cast were told about their cut in rations, Tim wasn't at all fazed by the news. It was also at this time that Larissa decided she wanted to leave. Tim did not believe her reasons for going: 'she said she had been a free spirit all her life and felt trapped here. I didn't accept that and told her that we made our own boundaries on this island.'

For Stuart, he had nothing but praise. 'He's a cracker of a bloke, he's lovely and has given a lot of people inspiration and enlightened others about gay people. If I don't get eaten or die of starvation, I'll definitely go and have a little dance with Stuart in Manchester when I get back.'

Name: Lisa Kastaniotis
From: **Victoria**   Age: **22**

A bit of a drama queen, Lisa is loud, vivacious and good fun. She was a real heroine during the selection process because of her climbing ability, even though she cried at the time because she is terrified of heights. But her determination and spirit won through. She was the first of the Aussies to bond with the group as a whole: they all liked and respected her sufficiently to vote her in as leader in their third week, the first of the girls to hold that position.

Lisa was also the first to notice the cultural differences between the Aussie girls and the Brits. 'I assumed we would be the same over women's rights', she commented, but she couldn't believe that it was mostly the boys who bought the drinks at the bar during their training days on Tonga. 'In Australia you would never get away with that.' So it was hardly surprising that she took great exception to the boys' banter, which developed into the sexism row. Lisa was the one who was most upset by the talk, weeping loudly, and when Andy tried to apologize, she turned on him. But when she had time to reflect she admitted that a lot of it stemmed from the fact that the Brits on the island had something that the Aussies didn't have: 'I guess they take comfort in the fact they can banter with each other, there's an underlying understanding that the three of us don't have. I woke up the following morning hoping that we could get over it; it was a sort of a breakthrough. It was a really horrible experience, but I think it helped me realize that there are differences and we aren't going to understand each other... now I feel I can step in and say I don't get it, rather than playing dumb and keeping quiet.'

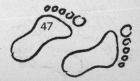

Lisa was the first person to make a first public apology for the misunderstanding, which gained her a lot of approval from the group.

She joined in with everything from building to fishing and, with Emma-Rosa, took charge of supplies; she was also one of the first to acknowledge that some people were not pulling their weight. While she enjoyed the responsibility, she also found it quite stressful – particularly as there was so little food: 'never in my life have I been so stressed about something you take for granted at home. Here, everything we do makes a difference, so that if we don't catch fish we have to dig into our rations... we all have to rely on our strengths and resources.'

Lisa bonded quite quickly with Stuart and the two of them became very close during their time together.

Although she and Larissa were very friendly with Lucy M, after about four weeks they began to distance themselves from her. 'We've even stuck up for her when she was wrong,' Lisa explains, 'but lately we're worried about her attitude and scared she'll drag us down with her, as she's lost all her friends apart from us. We can't stop being friends with her, because who knows what she might do, but we'll just cool it.'

Name: *Michael Lee*
From: **Hertfordshire**   Age: **20**
Luxuries: dirty cards, lyric pad and pen, ketchup

Known to his friends as Blough – and to others as the Gentle Giant – Michael is an unemployed musician/rapper. Although he is a qualified chef and has been a builder, Blough says music is his whole life. His other interests are sports and women. Dry, kind and humorous he is both perceptive and determined as well as being fiercely loyal and protective to his mum and eighteen-year-old sister, with whom he lives. He feels a lot of anger towards his father, whom he feels has never helped the family out and who comes and goes as he pleases. Blough feels his dad neither loves nor cares for the family – all of which is set out in his first rap, 'Daddy's Boy'. To try and get his dad to understand what he felt, Blough sent him a copy of the rap, but received no response. Six months before he went to the island, both Blough and his sister decided to cut their father out of their lives completely, and now he says he feels much better for it. Blough's sensitive side is well developed. He was worried about his mother's finances during his absence, as both he and his sister contribute to the household. He was also seriously concerned about his gran, who was very ill while he was on the island.

Blough was definitely 'one of the lads', teaming up with Kev and Andy for a laugh, and setting up their own camp at Cosa Nostra. However, a number of the girls also found him easy to talk to and sympathetic, although Lucy T said he scared her sometimes because he was so big! Blough quickly adapted to the island and was one of the few not to complain about the food (although in the end he lost about two stone in weight). 'I'm missing my family and friends but I am in no hurry to go back,' he revealed after three weeks. His only real fears were snakes and rats – he wasn't sure about how many of the former were about, but he knew that there were rats in the vegetable patch. Blough was thrilled to be chosen to take part in *Shipwrecked*, and loved his time on Nuku: 'I pinch myself every morning. The group is getting on really well and although I made a snap decision about Lucy T, I completely changed my mind after a couple of weeks, because she has turned out to be one of the nicest girls I've ever met.'

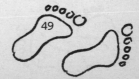

He was snogged by Larissa when she was drunk one night and explained that although he didn't really like her, she was great to look at and he wasn't going to say no! He got on really well with Vic and he was one of the few people she felt she could talk to naturally; indeed, he became very concerned about her, because even though he was hugely sympathetic, he did not know how to help her with her problems.

Blough was one of the few members of the cast who got on with everyone, which even surprised him, as he said he would never mix with such a bunch of people at home. Although thrilled that he was made leader in the eighth week, he was not happy with the responsibility: 'I'm not leader material. I thought I'd like it, but I don't – I just feel guilty all the time, feel as if I should be doing something constantly.' In spite of not being happy about his position, he was the only one to get the girls to dig the long-drop – which both astonished and impressed the rest of the lads.

Blough was the first to bridle against all the meetings and got really upset with Tim's attitude over the rum stealing. He felt he should have tackled the three lads rather than the group and was hurt that Tim felt Andy and Kev had betrayed the trust of the group and might have forfeited their right to go on the ration run. Finally, he realized the truth of what Andy had said to him, 'that no matter how well you think you know people, in the end you're on your own.'

But in the end Blough unreservedly loved the place and the experience. He hadn't had a holiday for twelve years and had never been away from home for longer than a week before being shipwrecked.

Name: LUCY MASGUD

From: **London**   Age: **22**

Luxuries: rainbow flag, gel, book, box of crisps

A mixed-race lesbian, Lucy is studying Politics at university and wants to pursue a career in politics when she has graduated. She is also a vegetarian and an animal rights activist and has been arrested twice for taking part in demonstrations against live animal exports, and she is active in gay issues. Lucy is no stranger to publicity, as she was in the Admiral Duncan bomb blast in Soho in 1999. Her girlfriend, Veronica, was working in the pub as a barmaid at the time – and both girls featured in press reports about the incident. The bombing caused the break-up of their relationship, as Veronica became very withdrawn and depressed in its aftermath. Lucy hasn't had a relationship since, and says that she cannot imagine finding anyone she could love as much again.

Lucy's sexuality is obviously a major issue for her and being a lesbian is a constant part of her conversation. She admits to being a bit of a big mouth and of having no fear in saying what she feels is right. And she doesn't balk at telling people if she doesn't like them.

At the interview Lucy stated that there could be nothing more boring than everyone getting on with each other, but there was little chance of that with her around. In fact, the first two major causes of friction on the island were brought about by her. The first row was about her rainbow flag, which some people did not want foisted on them; the second main crisis was when some girls, including Lucy, stole from crew camp. However, she provoked a humdinger when she took on one of the blokes – Tony – for being a sexist pig, which brought most people's disapproval onto her.

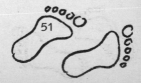

Lucy maintains that she didn't care, that she couldn't stand Tony and that she was right in her opinion of him.

She was not surprised to be chosen to be shipwrecked: 'I was the second girl, it was an odd feeling, neither happy or sad. But there were a number of people I would like to have been picked and I didn't think that the people I would be here with would be like this. Most of them are brain dead and not the sort of people I would hang around with in England.'

Lucy knows she is thought of as loud and aggressive and that a few people don't like her because they think she is stirring things all the time. 'I'm not a stirrer,' she argues, 'it's just that I don't like some of them and I can't be bothered to explain what's wrong with them.' Surprisingly, perhaps, once on the island she confessed, 'I'm on the verge of going home a lot, I'm very homesick.'

Lucy admits that she probably applied to be on the programme for all the wrong reasons: 'I was trying to get over my ex-girlfriend – it was a really miserable break-up. Also, it meant that if I got chosen I wouldn't have to work for the summer.'

And what is she hoping to get out of it? 'I'm hoping I might get a bit more nookie when I leave Nuku.'

Name: Samara Milford
From: **Wiltshire**   Age: **22**
Luxuries: pad of paper, book, garlic salt

Samara is a mixed-race bisexual and is used to home comforts and her own way. Currently training to be a Montessori nursery nurse, she also works part-time in a vodka bar. She is dating a much younger boy at the moment, and was considered very attractive by many of the boys at the final selection weekend.

Samara was one of the main instigators of the streaking at midnight and the game of spin-the-bottle on the Saturday night, but although she snogged a few people – boys and girls – she distanced herself as things got steamier and watched the antics from a distance.

Samara is a little spoilt – she still lives at home, but stated that she wanted to be picked so that she could break out from the comfort zone that has surrounded her all her life. She was quite convinced that she would be picked and took smug satisfaction from the fact that while her younger sister also applied for *Shipwrecked*, she didn't make it!

Samara is quite well travelled, as her father was in the army, and she lived in Belize for two years. Her hobbies are singing, writing poetry – she wrote a special poem for Lucy T's birthday – football and aerobics, which accounts for her putting on an impressive gymnastics display during the selection weekend!

For somebody who gives the impression of being so sure of herself, Samara went through a great deal of insecurity in the first couple of weeks, as she wasn't sure how the others saw her. And even though she was getting on very well with both Emma-Rosa and Jo, she went through a phase of not knowing whether they really liked her. She missed home, her boyfriend and cuddles and although she loved the island at times she was incredibly lonely and felt a fake. By the end, however, she found herself, 'Trying to imagine living without all these people twenty-four hours a day, seven days a week. It will be difficult with them not being there!'

Samara is a kind-hearted soul and was concerned about Vic's unhappiness on the island – as a gesture of friendship, she asked Vic to help her dye her hair pink for the punk party. This added to her rather exotic looks, which she has adorned with a tongue stud and a tattoo around her belly button.

Her competitive nature came to the fore during the island Olympics and she was thrilled to win the long jump. In fact, she was cross with Kevin, Jody and Emma for not taking the games seriously. She was pleased, through, when Emma told her that the boys thought she was quite cute, although she complained, 'I want to be foxy and sexy and always end up being cute.' But mostly, she felt that the boys took no notice of her and never listened to any of her suggestions. She would have loved to do the ration run and felt she had the stamina and ability to do it, but knew she had no chance of being picked – she found this the most frustrating aspect of being on the island.

Samara knew that there were rumours about Andy and herself. However, while admitting that they were attracted to each other, she maintained all along that nothing would happen because she was in love with somebody at home.

Name: *Joanne Mills*
From: **Hertfordshire**   Age: **21**
Luxuries: journal, book, I Ching

The archetypal blonde babe, but no airhead. Joanne is currently studying Marketing and Advertising in London, but says she is tired of judging and being judged on appearances. On the other hand, she loves fashion and design and anything that's hip. She also adores the works of Aldous Huxley and Friedrich Nietzsche. She has a massive dragon tattoo snaking all the way down her back and has had her nipples pierced as a birthday present for her boyfriend.

Throughout the ten weeks on the island Joanne always looked good and was constantly sewing and re-making the clothes she

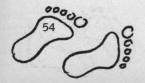

had brought with her. She also organized a fashion show and made most of the clothes used for it, using her ingenuity, some of her own pieces and items that the others had brought along. Joanne is currently dating a drummer, and says she is straight but likes to experiment. On the selection weekend she snogged a number of girls and boys; she thought Tim was the most attractive boy. She shared a tent that weekend with Tim and Jody, snogging each of them in turn and, according to some people, took things a lot further with Tim. She was also involved in a streaking and mooning session with the girls.

However, on the island Joanne was much more withdrawn and happier to observe than to join in. Each morning she did a work-out on the beach with Emma-Rosa and spent time perfecting her tan. But she was quite trenchant in her views. For instance, she was extremely angry when she discovered that Larissa and Lisa had been stealing food: 'I was totally shocked. These were people I trusted and all they did was cause terrible tension in the camp. I was angry because they only owned up because they knew they had been rumbled. These people have fallen in my estimation.'

Joanne was also critical of the way the Aussie girls overreacted to what she described as simply the boys' sexual banter: 'It must be because they still have to deal with sexual discrimination at home.' She got very angry with Lucy M for stirring the situation, 'I think Lucy M has a real nasty streak. She's a bit of a bitch who likes to be the centre of attention, which is why she causes trouble.' While Lucy thought that Jo was the most attractive person on the island, she also thought she was positively Neanderthal for taking tea to the boys when they were building a hut!

On the whole, though, Jo got on with most of the shipwrecked – she thought Tony was lovely and that Andy was the most fanciable man on the island. Jody she thought was nice

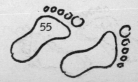

and intelligent, but she also felt that he didn't speak well in a group situation. When he was leader she said he moaned about people not using their initiative, 'but many can't because they don't know what to do. It's his job to tell them what to do – that's not delegation, that's management.'

And although she was one of the best-liked people in the group, Jo was one of the first to break away and go off to live on her own.

Name: *Victoria Oliver*
From: **Wolverhampton**   Age: **18**
Luxuries: hair dye, tobacco, mirror

The youngest member of the cast, Vic describes herself as a bisexual feminist punk. She's about to complete a two-year Art & Design course and works four nights a week in a nightclub to save funds for travelling. Until quite recently she lived at home, but has now moved out to houseshare with student friends.

Vic's looks are striking and innovative. She has a Tank Girl hairstyle – shaved at the sides with multicoloured dreads on top – and dresses in army fatigues or baby doll dresses, complete with stripy, laddered tights and Doc Marten boots. Money has always been tight, and Vic swears she would never spend more than five pounds on any item of clothing. She is also amazingly resourceful – she was the applicant who couldn't afford or get access to a video camera for her audition tape, but managed to persuade the manager of a local camera shop to use one of his display cameras and film her on the street outside the shop!

Although she is young, Vic appears very sure of herself and her views. A strong feminist, she thinks all macho lads are closet

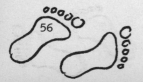

gays. She found it extraordinary that some people preferred talking to a camera than to any of the other cast. Her passion is punk, which she missed desperately from day one. And although she is a bit of a loner, she was incredibly popular with the rest of the cast, who were sad to see her go and still spoke of her with great affection right to the end of their stay.

After day four Vic knew she wanted to go home, but agonized for another two or three weeks before leaving. She felt incredibly guilty for being unhappy in such a beautiful place, especially as she had tried so hard to get there. 'I think my attitude sucks. I really thought I was more mature, but I am finding it really hard to be out of my own environment. I want to be in my own safe place where it's OK not to have a job or go to uni.' But despite her strong beliefs, Vic found that being among the group made her begin to question things about herself, which made her start feeling uncomfortable. 'It's nothing to do with them, it's to do with my own mentality, but they just make me feel so bad about myself, as if I'm stupid and could never accomplish anything.'

All of the others were concerned about Vic's unhappiness, which became increasingly obvious, and they tried hard to cheer her up. They even organized a punk party in her honour. Everyone was thrilled when after two weeks she said she'd decided to stay – but she left a week later. Vic's leaving underlined the homesickness that a lot of the cast were feeling – Stuart cried when she left, but admitted afterwards that he had done so more for himself than for her.

Vic's isolation was increased by the girliness of some of the girls and the sense of purpose of some of the lads. 'I don't really know what I'm doing. Perhaps that's why I'm so homesick, 'cos these people have made me realize that I don't know what I am doing with my life.' But she admits she has always been a loner, even at school.

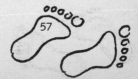

Name: *Lucy Taylor*
From: **Blackpool**   Age: **20**
Luxuries: penknife, diary, book

Loud, noisy and excitable, Lucy is reading Classics at University College, London. She comes across as quite childish and immature – even her mother, she says, is hoping that she will return from the experience a little more grown up. However, there is a more thoughtful, serious side to her. On her twenty-first birthday, which was celebrated on the island, she said that she realized for the first time that material things are not that important. That's why she loved the home-made cards and presents the rest of the cast made for her and why the poems written for and about her moved her deeply. However, the boisterous side soon emerged after a quantity of rum had been consumed. Lucy went swimming with her knickers on her head before falling asleep and throwing up into Tim's sleeping bag!

At home she likes horse-riding, snowboarding, sculpture and art, and has been involved with her boyfriend, James, for more than two and a half years. She freely admitted that she was a bit worried about leaving him for so long.

The one thing that Lucy said annoyed her about the last series of *Shipwrecked* was the constant moaning and whining, which is one of the reasons she got cross with the Aussie girls in the sexism row. Some of the others thought Lucy was overreacting to having chickens on the island after she gave them names and tried to stop them being cooked for dinner. In the end, she did eat some of the meat and admitted to having a lot of respect for the girls who tried to kill the

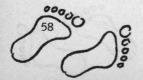

chickens: 'They at least involved themselves in the process, even though they couldn't carry it through.'

Lucy occasionally felt low because she believed that everybody thought of her as a dippy, cocky girl from Blackpool. She was hurt because she felt she was not respected and that her views were not taken seriously by anyone except for Jody, whom she thought was the only one who realized she had a brain. 'I may be dippy but I'm not thick,' she commented, ruefully.

When some of the lads tried to frighten the girls with tales of an escaping convict, seeing strange shadows and hearing voices in the night, Lucy was the one most spooked. In the end the boys had to stop because she was getting so scared.

After just two weeks, this very bubbly and bright girl began to feel incredibly alone: 'There's not one person I can turn to. It is very lonely and has made me question the very nature of the friendships we have formed – are they just for convenience?' Lucy analyzed what the ten-week duration would be like quite early on. She felt that during the first two weeks people would be elated, excited and get on. Then would come the middle section, when bits of their real characters began to show, the bits they tried to keep hidden, and only after that stage would the real friendships form.

Name: *Kevin Thomas*
From: **Lincolnshire**   Age: **18**
Luxuries: blow-up animal, mirror, rugby ball

The archetypal lad. Kevin is a sports student and part-time barman desperate to become famous – and the first thing he wanted to do when he returned was find an agent. But while

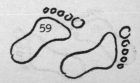

he loves being the centre of attention, and is loud and noisy, Kevin showed that he could be kind, caring and sensitive. He even cried when he was selected.

Kevin is fostered, but points out that he has looked after himself since he reached the age of eighteen. His parents split when he and his brother were young, and the boys stayed with their father. When he could no longer afford to keep them, they were fostered. After a few months he was able to get them back again – but soon after he was forced to give them up. Kev says the worst day of his life was seeing his father crying when he had to leave the boys for the second time.

Kevin split up with his girlfriend just before the selection weekend, but he missed her on the island and made her a video for her birthday – he said he had never felt as strongly about anyone in his life. And while he openly admitted to being homophobic and initially avoided Stuart during the selection weekend, he eventually ended up talking to him most of the evening and thought he was an OK guy. He also became very friendly with Beth, and she was one of the few people he talked to about his home life.

Kevin participated in every aspect of the training, but was one of the people most affected by the pig slaughter – in the end most people agreed with him and they decided not to take pigs to the island. However, he was fine about chickens and was one of the people who helped fish during their stay. He was very moved when he first saw a shark and was inspired to swim after it, because it was so scary and so beautiful. He even managed to get Lucy M on his side during the sexism debate – she felt that in spite of his moronic jokes he had a deep respect for women because of the way he talked about his girlfriend.

Although he claimed to like and admire Jody, Kevin became a little jealous when people always turned to Jody when they

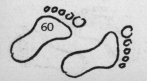

wanted something done rather than to him. He was desperate to do something for the group, which is why he was overwhelmed to be chosen for the ration run and then devastated when it looked as if he had jeopardized it by stealing some rum; for a while he was angry and inconsolable. Fortunately, everything calmed down when the lads were voted back in.

Name: *Larissa Walker*
From: **Queensland**   Age: **23**
Luxuries: diary, the book *Savages*

The Australian version of the *Baywatch* babe, Larissa is a former model who now works for a computer company. At the selection weekend she showed that she really liked to be the centre of attention. That was something the boys didn't mind because they thought she was great-looking, although the girls thought she was shallow, citing the fact that she constantly worried about her appearance.

On the island she got very close to Jody and they were often seen together on the beach or snuggled up in the hammock. However when she reported that he had kissed her she added, 'the earth did not move for me and I hope he doesn't do it again.' Quite early on she claimed that the *Shipwrecked* experience had taught her how to live with other people – 'we should look for the best in everyone and accept people as they are' – while stating that at home she wouldn't choose the rest of the cast as her friends.

At one stage she became very worried about her health – she got sunstroke, heatstroke, was losing weight and felt nauseous all the time: 'I was quite scared 'cos I had no energy and thought

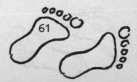

it was the cause of malnutrition.' However, a number of the cast thought much of this was simply attention seeking. Larissa's main friends were Lisa, Tony, Jody and Lucy M, although she tried to distance herself from the latter after the sexism row – she claimed that Lucy was putting words into her mouth.

Larissa got fed up with the way the whole island was run after about three weeks, claiming it was all about the group 'and nothing about the individual.' 'Yesterday we were given a lecture on how to go to the toilet! I've been living on my own since I was seventeen and I find some of these attitudes offensive. I feel as if I'm just doing time here, as if my life is on hold.' And it was these sentiments that in the end informed her decision to leave the island, plus the fact that she felt she could no longer live with the restrictions of the camera. Most of the rest of the cast neither believed nor were sympathetic to these views, feeling that Larissa loved the camera and always performed for it. However, none of them were sufficiently interested in keeping her and eventually became bored with the way she constantly postponed her leaving date.

She came to believe the sexism row was a cultural misunder-standing after Jo, Tim and Emma talked her through what the boys were doing. 'Once we understood that we were fine, but Lucy carried on about Tony being sexist.' However, in general she felt all three of them had adapted to being in the minority quite well. 'There were some language problems to begin with, and some different references – the Brits have quite different TV shows.' But of the three she felt that D was the one outsider, while 'Lisa has really surprised me – she has been really strong.'

Although Larissa admits that it was her best friend's idea that she should try for the show, 'It was something I always wanted to do – to see if I could survive without all the things I like living with.' However, way down the line she surprised herself by

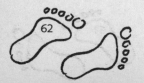

saying that she would miss the people, rather than the place, when she got home: 'I think I will go back a stronger person and much more tolerant of people and more appreciative of simple things like a toilet!'

She was quite concerned about being away from her boyfriend Aaron, whom she had been with for about eight months. Indeed, one of the reasons she was against anything happening with Jody was because her relationship with Aaron was still a bit rocky and she did not want anything to upset him 'because we have a lot of issues still to resolve.'

ISLAND LEADERS

Week 1 *Tony*

Week 2 *Jody*

Week 3 *Lisa*

Week 4 *Andy*

Week 5 *Stuart*

Week 6 *Tim*

Week 7 *Beth*

Week 8 *Blough*

Week 9 *'Victoria'*

WEEK 1

Monday *On Pangaimotu learning to fish*

Tuesday *Trip to Nuku cancelled because of weather*

Wednesday *At last — shipwrecked!*

Thursday *Tony elected leader, make-shift shelter started*

Friday *Rations found*

Saturday *Work on proper shelter*

Sunday *Rice and corned beef*

In a state of high excitement, near-hysteria and (for some) extreme hangover fatigue, the fourteen members of the British cast arrived in the Kingdom of Tonga on 17 August 2000, ready to test their nerve, will-power and survival instincts to the full. For the next ten weeks, they would be living on the deserted island of Nuku as shipwreckees, with just a modicum of rations and few home comforts. Not an easy task for a group of people brought up in an age of fast food, state-of-the-art communication, central heating, twenty-four hour television, DVDs and aeroplanes – not to mention flushing lavatories, running water and switch-on, switch-off relationships. None of them had lived in an isolated community before, let alone had to forage for food, and of course they were all used to choosing their own friends and intimates. Here, they would be bunched together with people they hardly knew, and with whom they had little in common. People, in fact, whom they had only just met and with whom they had to live in close proximity for the next seventy days. They were also about to be joined by three Australians who were already on the flight from Sydney, filled with excitement about the adventure and foreboding about the 'whingeing Poms' they had seen on the first series of *Shipwrecked*, and hoping that the cast of the new series would be a bit more practical. Although held together by the bonds of nationality and the paucity of their number, the Aussies were as different from each other as it was possible to be: Dharma (otherwise known as D), the all-out outward-bound Oz male; Larissa, the pretty blonde who loved the camera; and Lisa, the noisy drama queen.

In due course, their fears were allayed by the welcoming party awaiting them at the airport. The Brits, already overwhelmed by the sunshine and smiles of Tonga, were prepared to love every-body forever in this tropical paradise… or were they? Over the next few days of training in basic survival skills, their disparate

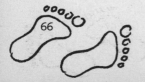

characters and different aims began to show through.

While still enjoying the luxury of getting to know each other on the first day, they were able to relax and recover from the long flight. After that, every morning brought coaching and practical advice on what they needed to master in order to survive the rigours of an island without readily available food and water. Their teacher was a local man called Ernie, who had exceptional communication skills, an easy-going manner and a ready smile. With his son Norris and friend John, he took the seventeen rookies and demonstrated how to light a fire and build an umu (an oven dug into the ground, which is the traditional Tongan way of cooking). As in any group activity, some people paid more attention than others, which would lead to friction later on when there was cooking to be done and most of the cast had forgotten how to light a fire. Of course, the one or two who could do it then had to be around at the start of mealtimes – a state of affairs that only underlined D's initial prejudices about the Brits being useless and lazy…

The nearby island of Atata became their school for survival when they went off with Ernie to spend a day learning how to find and prepare food. Shinning up a coconut tree looks a doddle when done by an expert, but when attempted by our fearless castaways it was initially nothing short of a shambles. Some wouldn't even try it, opting instead to develop another skill that could be of communal use. The three boys who later became known as 'the lads' – Kevin, Andy and Blough – treated it like a fairground game until an exhausted Blough bowed out, leaving the other two to make a number of dodgy ascents. Aussie Lisa, who had already battled her fear of heights at the selection weekend, decided she didn't need to climb a coconut palm… ever! Stuart soon emerged as the champion coconut-fetcher, using all his dancer's training, agility and sense of balance to race up and

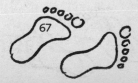

down the trunks like a natural – to the delight of the Brits. All that remained was for him to stand still long enough to chop one or two up.

But not all food gathering is fun. Some of it demands nerve and skill, and for a generation used to seeing their meat pre-packed or ready-cooked, finding it while it was still on the hoof or wing was a highly traumatic experience. The only one not participating, and therefore not affected, was Lucy M – surprisingly, the only vegetarian on the island. None of them enjoyed the prospect of killing to eat, although they all understood that it was something they would simply have to do in order to survive. For the first time since they got together, there was virtually silence while Ernie and Norris showed them how to butcher, pluck and clean a chicken.

It was the pig killing that they really bonded over, however. A few of the cast decided that they really couldn't watch what was happening and left the scene; those who stayed on were profoundly affected by what they witnessed. For days afterwards, Victoria kept saying how guilty she felt about watching the process, while tough guy Kev was appalled by it and had to walk away. 'I used to be a butcher,' he explained, 'but I didn't like seeing it scared, and I certainly didn't like hearing it squeal.' And though all the cast enjoyed the pork when it was cooked, they decided there and then that they didn't want any pigs brought to the island, as none of them really had the stomach for slaughter. To sighs of relief, they were also shown how to weave palm fronds together for the walls and roof of their shelter. Perhaps not surprisingly, the girls showed a greater aptitude for this than many of the boys – much to the disgust of the Aussies, who felt that the girls should be more robust and take on harder work.

It was a lot to take in for one day, so the bar provided a welcome release when they got back to the main island that

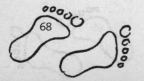

evening. The following day was Sunday, a day for resting, and also for church, which many of them visited. Monday saw the cast on another nearby island, Pangaimotu, where they were taught how to fish for supplies and handle a boat through deeper waters to explore the surrounding sea and islands. They had been informed that each of them was allowed to spend one night away from Nuku at the little neighbouring island of Fukave – either on their own or with one other member of the cast, with no cameras around. The idea was so enticing that they all worked hard at mastering the canoe, believing it to be the only means of getting to the island. (They realized later that the stronger ones could actually swim there.)

Excitement was running pretty high at base camp that evening, because in the morning the experiment proper would begin. But nature decided to take a hand in events and they woke to heavy skies and the rumbling of thunder. Their first experience of a tropical storm was going to keep them away from their slice of paradise for another twenty-four hours.

The following morning's brilliant blue skies saw the cast heading for the gap in the reef and their new home for the next ten weeks. None of them was quite prepared for what they saw as they approached Nuku – after talking and dreaming about it for so long, the first sighting was a mix of high excitement and overwhelming emotion. 'I couldn't jump off the boat and swim ashore like the others for quite some time,'

'I just stood and looked at it for ages. It was the most beautiful thing I had ever seen.'
Kevin

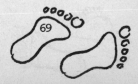

confessed Emma-Rosa, 'because for the first time the reality of our situation hit me. There was this perfect island in the middle of the sea and nothing else around. All I could think of was whether I was going to be able to last the course or not.' Before losing her nerve, she felt the only thing to do was to get out of the boat and onto the shore with everyone else; within minutes they were all splashing in the surf or running along the beach. One of the reasons Nuku was chosen as the location for the series was because it's supposed to have the best beaches in Tonga. It might have seemed par for the course to the three Australians, but to the fourteen Brits, who had just left a dreary, damp summer, it was a dream come true.

However, bravado came to the fore the minute Ernie's boat disappeared over the horizon (although there was a camera crew on the island, they were only there to film), and the cast were left to their own devices at last. Tony was voted in as the island's first leader. On the main island, they had discussed how they would elect each week's leader, and several names were mentioned as possibilities, though never Tony's. On the other hand, Jody, whose name had cropped up time and time again, had to wait until week two before he got his chance. 'It was just as well, really. I think my form of leadership was just a little too laid-back for the first week when we really needed to get stuck in with most of the heavy work,' he admitted later.

There was tropical loveliness all around, but it soon became apparent that food and shelter had to be the first priorities. A recce party quickly discovered supplies (rice, tins of meat, vegetables and coffee), while Tony asked Lisa and Emma-Rosa to be in charge of rations and food, much to Australian Lisa's relief. She'd watched the Poms in the first series stealing food, and was already worried that it would happen this time around too.

While the guys, Lucy M and Lucy T got on with building a

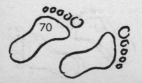

temporary shelter and exploring the island, the girls and Stuart began weaving as well as getting their first real chance to work on their suntans. They dragged the palm fronds down to the beach where, equipped with their newly acquired survival skills and lashings of sun screen, they began making walls and a roof for their new home.

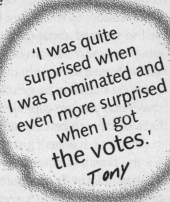

'I was quite surprised when I was nominated and even more surprised when I got the votes.'
Tony

By sunset, a temporary shelter was in place, an umu had been dug in and the first of the cast's own meals was underway. They soon discovered that food took much longer to put together and cook using such a primitive oven – even a cup of coffee took at least twenty minutes each morning, and after a few days the spartan conditions had a number of the cast pining for the conveniences of home. 'Oh, for a toaster,' Stuart sighed, wistfully.

But the experiment had only just begun. The food was bland and later on there was rarely enough of it, but in those first few heady days most people just downed their rice and corned beef and were grateful for it. Australian Larissa was the first to bemoan the meagre rations, declaring that she was bound to fall ill from malnutrition and vitamin deficiencies because back home she was used to eating up to six meals a day! After three days, Emma-Rosa was worried about the lack of fresh fruit (this was before they discovered the island was awash with papaya trees), and on day four, Vic was complaining that she was bored with rice. By the next mealtime, several people were complaining about Emma-Rosa's bossiness – telling them what to eat and how many crackers

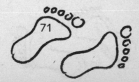

to take – while Lisa was beginning to feel the pressure of her responsibilities by the end of the first week: 'Never in my life have I felt so stressed about something you take for granted at home. Tonight we only had sweet potato left, and if we don't catch any fish we'll have to dig into our rations – all of this means we have to rely on ourselves to get through. But it does make you realize how much you are capable of. There's so little food and choice that you have to be creative.'

Of course, it wasn't just the food that took some getting used to – the time had come to get on with the day-to-day business of living. All the fun of learning on the main island had been spent in relative privacy and comfort under a proper roof with a flushing lavatory and running water. Under the stars at Nuku

LISA

Best:
Sleeping on the beach and looking up at the millions of stars.

Birthday parties!

Snorkelling along the reef.

Getting to know a crazy bunch of Brits – and actually forming friendships!

Always being challenged, both mentally and physically.

Worst:
The long-drop. I just can't express how distressing this experience was!

RICE! Two or three times a day for sixty-six days. I nearly went mad.

Thunderstorms. Fearing that the house would blow away.

Dirty clothes and salty skin.

No contact with family and friends.

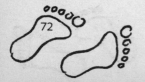

it was all very different... First, there was the long-drop – the camp lavatory – which had to be re-dug every week, swarming with flies and the smell of seventeen people's excreta. The only lavatory paper was something that Tim dubbed the 'Andrex bush', a plant with large, non-slippery leaves. And then there were the dormitory arrangements – rows of sleeping bags and palm-leaf mattresses lined up next to each other. Anyone could see by that stage that not everything on the island was going to be rosy.

Although the permanent shelter was put up within days, with every one of the guys working flat out, the proximity of strangers didn't take long to take its toll. Firstly, the group became divided between the night owls and those who went to bed early and didn't appreciate the late-night chats down on the beach or under the stars, claiming that the noise kept them awake. Then there was the farting, which kept the Brits hugely amused, much to the chagrin of the Aussies, who were unfamiliar with the great British tradition of scatological humour... Combine the noise and smell of the passing wind with the bad jokes, and poor D was crawling up the palm fronds with despair.

'I wouldn't choose any of these people to be my friends at home.'
Larissa

Ultimately, it was the snoring that caused the first outburst – it was bad enough being kept awake by voices and laughter, but then the minute certain people finally fell asleep, the snores began to ring out loud and clear. Stuart and a couple of the girls were the first to vent their irritation, and although several of the

castaways tried to sleep on the beach, they were driven back into the shelter by the vicious and indiscriminate mosquitoes. And if the mosquitoes didn't get you, the hermit crabs did, as Lucy T discovered when she woke up one morning with her sleeping bag covered in them.

Through the eyes of the hut-cam (the secret camera the cast were able to tell their worries and anxieties to in private), it soon became apparent that other things were amiss as well. Vic was already so homesick and unhappy that she was seriously thinking about going home, but was also feeling extremely guilty about complaining in such a beautiful place. Meanwhile, both Jo and Emma-Rosa were finding it hard to be away from home.

The first real trouble came about when Lucy M decided to put up her rainbow flag, the symbol of gay pride, by the shelter. It had been one of her three luxuries and she was determined it should fly. She had asked a number of people privately whether they objected, and when none of them did, she set about putting it up, but not before a heated discussion broke out. Kevin, who admitted on the island of Tonga that he had never met or mixed with any gay people before, was one of the most concerned, and some of the others felt she was deliberately flying the flag just to be provocative. As the only other gay cast member, Stuart was ambivalent about the whole thing: 'If it makes her feel better, that's OK, but I really don't want a big flag in my face reminding me about how different I am from everyone else. I don't see it as a difference. In my experience, flags have always been used to separate people.' Tony's only comment was about its design: 'Couldn't the gay community think of a slightly less garish flag? It is pretty revolting,' while Lucy T couldn't understand the fuss. 'It is,' she reminded everyone, 'only a piece of material.' Jody took a more personal view about the issue: 'I just think it's arrogant to put a flag up and expect everyone to

be happy about it, and I think Lucy knows that. I think she put it up in the end just to piss people off and to get noticed.' The one person who kept out of the discussion completely was Emma-Rosa, who confessed: 'I come from Belfast and there you see how flags are used and what they do to people.' Lucy, however, was not to be deterred, and the flag went up on one side of the hut.

'We are Aussies and we don't whinge.'
D

Around the same time, other cracks were appearing. D in particular was worried that the Poms weren't necessarily keeping up – 'How can you tell when a plane load of Poms has landed? The engine has stopped but the whining continues.' Brotherly (and sisterly) love was looking distinctly shaky by the end of the first week on Nuku.

It took the pragmatic Kev to bring everything back into focus: 'It's not as easy as everyone thinks. It's hot, we haven't got much food – and what we have people don't like – and it's hard work. The mosquitoes are biting, the floor is hard, the house has to be finished, the boat has to be repaired, the toilet is awful, the heat is making people go funny, everyone is cutting and injuring themselves and yet we've all been given one of the greatest gifts – [a stay] on one of the most beautiful places on Earth.'

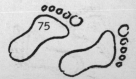

LUCY T'S DIARY

I am writing this in New Zealand, in the hotel, and my bed might not be comfy enough. I feel dizzy from the plane and my ear doesn't hurt much! The flight was so long. I have no concept of time and it feels like those days have not even existed. Fly to Tonga at 8pm 2nite, then stay there for three days to train and then to the island, apparently it's AMAZING. Getting really excited now, and now it's only started to hit me. I love all that outdoor stuff, at least nobody will be all FASHION FASHION blah blah make-up – can't be arsed with all that stuff. God, I want a bed on the island and my phone; no way am I letting rats piss on me and chew my sleeping bag.

Have arrived in Tonga now. We are all knackered and we thought our crap rickety little plane would crash. I am shaking and feel like I am still on the plane. My ribs and back are sore from, like, 4 million days of travelling. Go to the island in two days. CAN'T WAIT – it's meant to be beautiful. Staying in these little hut/house things (I'm with Emma, Samara and Vicky) and these huts R so cute – all surrounded by loads of plants & all the crickets are chirping, it's wicked. I can't believe I'm here, it's surreal. I feel quite emotional, probably because I'm totally cattle trucked, but I saw this guy today & at a glance he looked like Daddy; I miss him and Mum loads. No contact for so long, it's weird, but I need to grow up.

When we got off the plane in Tonga we were all filmed & we each got given a garland of flowers over our necks, it was wicked. I felt important and it was nice.

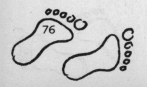

It really is paradise here. No hut yet, but we've put up this blue hut thing. Good job too, 'cos it totally pissed down all night. Tony was voted leader and I am secretary (v. important and privileged). I feel like I've been away for weeks. Our island is gorgeous, but it's much more gardeny and leafy than the last one. Haven't really taken into consideration the rain and all the snoring, not to mention the spiders and lizards – the place is swarming with them.

Just going for a bath in the sea with Beth and Stu. Just washed my clothes in the sea with weird soap. I slept so badly last night – so many different types of snoring in our tent, with loads of bugs.

At the moment I am sunbathing with Lisa, Larissa and Vicky, in our topless part [of the island] and my body so wants to fall asleep. God, I am sooo itchy, it's horrible. This never crossed my mind when I applied for [the programme] in England. Everyone seems to be getting on really well at the mo, it's cool, but a lot harder than I imagined… still feels a bit like a school trip, but I hope I'll get used to it. Not into the whole toilet thing at all – flies storming it & it's only day two. NO BOG ROLL SUCKS too.

It's been so hot today, everyone's been in a bad mood because we are all so fuzzy & dehydrated & hot. I'm so hungry, you take so much for granted (Ribena and ice and no mosquitoes!). I hope I last. My happiness goes in waves: sometimes I feel so good and so grateful to be here, but I kind of want to torture myself in order to get loads out of it. Worst bit of all was when we got off the boat for the first time & it drove away – fear just swept over me.

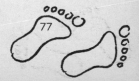

WEEK 2

Monday *Kept awake all night by snoring*

Tuesday *Skived on the beach.*

Wednesday *Shelter structure almost finished*

Thursday *Weaving palms for walls and roof*

Friday *Jody elected leader*

Saturday *Food horrible - rice and rice*

Sunday *A day of rest*

Nuku may be one small island, but demarcation lines were already being drawn halfway through the first week. The first separate area was not established by design – it happened more by accident. The girls used part of a beach to do all the palm weaving for the walls of the hut and for screening the long-drop. They chose that part of the beach because it gave them space to spread out, but much more importantly, it was the ideal place to work on their suntans. And to most of them it was pointless wearing bikini tops… An action that would hardly cause a raised eyebrow on any beach in Europe suddenly had all the chaps behaving a little like Victor Meldrew. According to Andy, the topless weaving meant the girls were making a statement that had the knock-on effect of making the lads feel like perverts, while others claimed that they felt intimidated by the activity. Consequently, the boys gave the area a wide berth. In retaliation, they set up a private beach area of their own, named the Beautiful Man Beach, which was 'to allow us to get away from their nagging'. No woman was allowed in this area unless accompanied by a beautiful man!

The girls reacted with almost complete indifference to the news, apart from Victoria, who demanded to know, 'Where are all the beautiful men? I haven't noticed any.' Within hours, Beth was found washing in this private area and was forced by the guys to apologize to all the men at lunch! The Aussies, particularly Lisa, were nonplussed by such behaviour – they were still having great difficulty coming to terms with the British sense of humour. Each day the demarcation lines between what they found acceptable and how the Brits behaved was becoming more and more defined. It wasn't just a shared sense of humour that was missing, but also any shared cultural experiences, such as TV programmes, bands, drinks and comedians. The Brits were hardly aware of any differences,

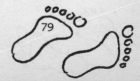

although they did occasionally bring in references to *Neighbours* to keep the Australians in the conversation! (Tim apologized later on for his truly awful grasp of Aussie slang and his accent.) Meanwhile, D was still concerned that too many Brits were swinging the lead and not doing the amount of work they should have been. Indeed, one of the first problems that Jody, as leader for week two, had to deal with, was Lisa still fretting over the work she had to do with the food.

This crisis occurred because Emma-Rosa, with whom Lisa shared the cooking, was teaching Jo aerobics and every morning the two of them, accompanied by Stuart, headed off for the beach, leaving Lisa to start breakfast on her own. After a few days this became too much for her and tears were shed. Jody made a decision that others had to help and two people were then volunteered to do each meal, with breakfasts going to Beth and Lucy T – although whoever got up first and was desperate for tea or coffee usually went to find wood and started a fire.

But in smaller ways too, chinks were beginning to appear. After the euphoria of arrival and the excitement of establishing a settlement for themselves, the subject of the lack of privacy reared its ugly head again. People were gradually becoming aware of the need for some space of their own. It wasn't so pronounced on days when the sun was shining and the group could be on the beach, swimming out to the reef or to the next island, doing a spot of fishing, weaving or reading. However, on overcast and rainy days, seventeen voices all clamouring to be heard in the confines of the shelter became too much for some. At one stage, a certain cast member pointed out that while some of the castaways were on the island because they wanted to be, others were there simply because they wanted to be on TV.

And it was during that second week that Jody, one of the more sensitive members of the cast, began to worry about whether the

others thought he was a recluse. His concern was brought on b[...]
Larissa observing that he was one of the quietest people on the
island. Jody confessed that he was getting to the point where he
was hankering after his own personal space 'because I find I go a
bit mad if people are around all the time'. Likewise, Tim confided
to the hut-cam that it was a struggle to get any space among
seventeen people, expressing a feeling common to everyone in
the group that would only grow stronger as time went on.

However, things begin to look up with the news that the
island's first VIP visitors were about to descend
on the cast: Ernie was bringing five
chickens as that week's luxury. In
honour of the occasion, Jody
made a special coop for them.
Each week the group was
given a choice of three
luxuries and they voted for
the one they wanted most.
And although fresh fish was
fantastic – if enough was
caught – and rice and vegetables was bearable when
supplemented with cans of corned
beef or mackerel, the cast was beginning
to hunger for meat. Lucy T's kind heart came to the fore when
she devised a plan to save the chickens from the pot. She believed
that if she befriended the birds and talked to them they would
relax and start laying eggs, thereby proving themselves much more
valuable alive than dead. Lucy decided not to speak out against
the plans because she felt that nobody would ever listen to her.
She was right. The camp's blood was up, and in spite of her views
and actions – she even gave the chickens names – two were

'You're
lonelier
among people
than you ever are
on your own.'
TIM

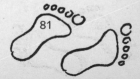

estined for dinner that first evening, proving that a bird in the pot is better than one in the coop.

Most people had helped clean and gut the fish they caught, no matter how squeamish they might have felt or how unpleasant the task was, but killing, plucking and drawing the birds proved a little more difficult. Andy and Blough rose to the challenge and volunteered, with Blough being the first to go for the chop. The more timid among them, such as Tony and Lisa, hid behind a tree while the deed was done. However, everybody was thrilled with the feast that was dished up later, even though two chickens among sixteen people could hardly be described as generous, and Lucy T lost her qualms sufficiently to tuck in. To continue their feasting some rum was cracked open and an impromptu party took place on the beach – it's amazing what a little protein can do…

Unfortunately, such high spirits were not to last. Daylight brought with it one of the most bitter episodes to take place throughout the ten weeks in paradise, one that was to split the group almost irrevocably. Like most major rows it started with a misunderstanding and again highlighted the differences between the Brits and the Aussies. Three of the guys – Andy, Tony and Kevin – were idly chatting near the two Aussie girls and Lucy M, who were also talking amongst themselves. Gradually the girls stopped to listen to what the men were saying and could not believe the way they were talking about women. 'We were just joking around, sure it was immature but it was neither offensive nor meant to be so.' Well, maybe, but when such topics as hormones and the menstrual cycle were touched on… Lucy M claimed that although the jokes started off as fairly mild, they became heavier and heavier, until the Aussie girls simply couldn't cope with any more of what they considered to be rampant sexism and misogyny. Lisa stomped off and Larissa retired, hurt, to the shelter.

Lucy M then accused the boys of being very aware of how wound up they were getting Larissa but continuing to make her more so by raising their voices so she could hear them in the shelter. 'They were definitely getting a kick out of it, but I'm not sure they realized how badly she was taking it,' she commented afterwards. 'What they were saying didn't offend me because there is always a lot of sexist banter between the boys and girls on the island and sometimes it can be quite a giggle, but really this time they were a bit over the top. Even Kevin said afterwards that he wouldn't say the things he was saying if his girlfriend were around.'

When Lisa returned after a cooling down walk she went to the shelter to talk to Larissa, who reported all. Then, both started to cry and threatened to leave the island, to the amazement of the guys. Andy began to apologize, only to be yelled at ferociously by Lisa. Kevin watched dumbstruck as Andy walked off to start cooking, chilling his fury with a little light vegetable chopping, while Tony went off in disgust, calling Lisa and Larissa 'two silly little girls'. Within seconds the whole island was buzzing with the news of the row. Jo, Emma-Rosa and Tim tried to calm the girls down, explaining it was meant to be a bit of a joke. Eventually, the situation became calmer. Lisa apologized to the guys and Tony apologized for the guys. But the outburst really left its mark. 'I cannot understand how something so blatantly a joke can be taken so

'To be honest I couldn't care less if they went home.'
Andy

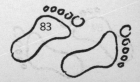

seriously,' Andy mused. 'The whole thing is ridiculous and unnecessary, but for the good of the group I'm going to act like nothing's happened.'

The Brits sided with each other. 'I thought it was pathetic,' Lucy T commented. 'I like the Aussie girls but it annoyed me that they overreacted. It's not like we're Martians and they're humans. I don't think the lads did anything wrong, it was a complete joke and they went over the top. But I'm glad Lisa apologized.' For his part, Kevin thought that the incident marked the start of problems on the island: 'We were blatantly joking but I've noticed that all these little irritations and upsets are girl orientated, none of the lads have any problems with each other. I'm really glad that Lisa stood up and apologized, but I think Larissa comes across as a bit of a drama queen.'

Jo was also convinced that the Australian girls totally over-reacted: 'I think the whole thing is a cultural thing. I have never felt sexually discriminated against growing up in Britain and because of that I'm able to joke about it. But the Aussies really reacted to the boys' banter so the only conclusion that I can draw is that in Australia they must still have to deal with sexual discrimin-ation. It must be a touchy subject for them to overreact to stupid jokes. But in the end I felt sorry for both sides – the girls because it must have been such a shock to encounter such obscenities, and the boys, who were astonished by the girls' threat of leaving the island.'

While the aftertaste hung about for most of the cast, Lisa was determined to put the whole thing behind her, calling it 'a slight misunderstanding with the boys.' But it did leave her pondering the differences between the two nationalities. 'I woke up this morning hoping we could get over it all and I think we can. There's been a breakthrough, first a really horrible experience but probably productive in the long term. We both now realize that we aren't going to understand each other but we can discuss it . When first came here I never thought there would be any real cultural differences, but they have an underlying understanding that we don't have. It's a shame really, because I didn't want there to be differences, but at least now we can acknowledge them.'

However, the saga does not end there. For later, during the evening of the incident, Tony and Jody took Larissa for a walk along the beach where they told her of Lucy M's part in the proceedings. Lucy M had been with the two Aussie girls at the start of the banter and when Larissa went into the shelter Lucy stayed outside. Every so often she popped in to see how Larissa was and to tell her what else the lads were saying. Both Jody and Tony maintained that this was all exaggerated and that Lucy was stirring things for reasons of her own. This news completely perplexed Larissa, and made her even more concerned. 'I'm not sure I can believe Lucy now,' she admitted. 'I feel torn not knowing if either of them are telling the truth. I like Tony and Lucy a lot and don't want it to come between any of us, but now there is a rift. I want us all to get along like we did before all of this happened. Lisa is alright and has cleared her head and realized that it was a joke for them even if it wasn't for us.'

'We started off so well, but things are beginning to deteriorate.'
Kevin

But Tony couldn't let go of it either. He spent the evening brooding about the incident and then confessed in the hut-cam that he had found out someone had been making more trouble about it, with particular reference to him. 'One thing bothered

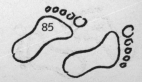

...e throughout the whole incident: I couldn't see what could be taken so seriously about what we had said. For some reason, Lucy lesbian has started up some bizarre hate campaign particularly against me. What she is doing is premeditatively evil and utterly bizarre. I found out that she had actually lied about things I was supposed to have said. I have told both Lisa and Larissa this but I am not going to make a song and dance about it. I am not going to confront her, but I have no doubt this will backfire on her and make her look really stupid.'

According to Tony, Lucy M had told a number of people, including the camera crew, that he had an on-screen as well as an off-screen personality and that off-screen he was a genuine sexist. When confronted by the crew about it, Tony admitted he was genuinely upset. 'This really bothers me, because I'm quite sensitive and when I think I've upset people I take it to heart. I know that I have friends in this group and that the girls like me just as much as the boys... they all know I am not a sexist and it's the first time in my life that I've been accused of being one.'

His views about Lucy were strengthened by Jody, who told of going into the shelter to check on Larissa only to hear Lucy M tell her that the boys really meant what they were saying and that they were all incredibly sexist. 'In my opinion Lucy doesn't come out of this well. I know stuff about her that proves she can be a pretty unpleasant person and can be pretty vindictive... within the first week she broke into the main camp and stole some food. Now I know she really can't be trusted and I'm worried about who she is going to pick on next. It could be me.'

So, slowly, the thin veneers of friendship were beginning to unpeel. Rows, lies and tales all played their part in making people suspicious and wary of each other. Larissa had found out about Lucy M stealing from crew camp and told Jody, whom she grew very close to over the weeks. Lucy herself had complained to Tony

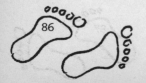

when he was leader that Emma-Rosa had been stealing tins of mackerel from their own food supplies – in that instance Tony had chosen not to believe her, because there was no evidence. But Jody, the nice guy, the hardest worker and Tony's closest friend, was feeling more and more concerned for his mate.

'He is extremely upset and confused about why she is picking on him. I feel really sorry for him, 'cos he has taken it to heart, but I'm sure she is sleeping fine,' he fumed. 'It needs someone to burst her bubble and to say that she can't be trusted. She has been continually antagonistic to a certain number of people. She may not like Kevin 'cos of the way he speaks, or how he has been brought up, or the fact he's a man, but she's as outwardly arrogant and nasty to him [in fact, Lucy calls him 'moron man'] as she is to Emma.'

And so it rumbled on until Tony could take no more and decided to confront Lucy with all the things she had been saying about him, in front of the group. Suddenly the whole camp joined in, with everyone shouting and slagging everyone else off, and before they knew it huge divisions were opening up between the group. The whole scene made Emma-Rosa sick, particularly as she was brought into it with the mackerel stealing. 'She had me in tears,' she said of Lucy M. 'I really can't believe a girl like that could make me cry; I think she's evil.' Lisa, despite her protestations of friendship with Lucy M, didn't speak in her defence, confessing afterwards that 'I feel particularly bad for not defending Lucy, she has been a really good friend to me on this island but I don't think she should have made such an assumption about Tony. She has only known him for a short while. Her judgment is unfair when we don't know each other very well.' Lucy T felt the whole thing was pathetic: 'I really like Lucy, although I don't think she was right, but she has shown that she is not afraid to be herself.'

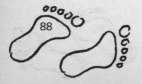

'Emma may not be my favourite person, but Lucy is extremely rude to her.'
Jody

Such sentiments were echoed by Kev: 'I felt a bit sorry for her, but she did bring the whole thing on herself. But you have to admire her. She is not afraid to stand up and defend herself; she's stubborn and she believes she is always right... on the other hand, she really upset Tony. She hasn't liked him from the beginning and used this as an opportunity [to get at him]. She's upset a number of people. She's not working within the group; she is not even making an effort. I don't want ten weeks of arguing, I'd rather see her leave if she's going to carry on like this.'

But according to Lucy T, the argument only strengthened Lucy M's resolve to stay on the island – out of spite. In fact, Lucy T reserved her anger for those so-called friends of Lucy M who didn't speak up for her when the chips were down. 'It's crap that some people sat there and listened to everyone slagging her off and then sidled up to her afterwards saying they really respected her.' She was particularly cross with Larissa, who had walked away in disgust, although Lucy had got herself into the argument by trying to stand up for the Australian girls.

'I don't want someone like this on this island.'
Kevin

Tony decided that there wasn't going to be a rapprochement: 'Let her do what she wants,' he commented, 'I am not going to get upset by her any more, I refuse to let her ruin my fantasy paradise. I'll try to be courteous but couldn't care less if she stays or goes, for the majority of the group and everyone in their right mind knows what she is like and what she is up to. I've never met anyone like her in my entire life. She is Beelzebub as far as I'm concerned. She should be committed, and I told her that last night. She wants to be a politician, but she's got no votes on this island. Christ, if I saw her name on a ballot paper, I'd draw some horns on it and send it to straight to Satan.'

So at last the devil had appeared in the Garden of Eden! It was left to Beth to plead for peace and understanding. 'I really, really wish people would stop arguing. It is such a paradise that surely we can all shut up for ten weeks.' But then Beth discovered a new problem: real, live rats, and they were in the vegetable garden that she so lovingly tended each day...

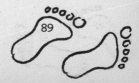

THE SOUTH PACIFIC

Most people know what the South Pacific looks like – we've all seen lots of photographs. And of course, there are the advertisements, promoting everything from the inimitable Bounty bar to the coconut liqueur Malibu. And then there are the movies, from the mouth-watering *Blue Lagoon* landscapes to *Mutiny on the Bounty* and *Castaway*. We can describe what any of these places look like in an instant – white sands, clear blue seas, bright sunshine, coconuts, palm trees, grass huts, grass skirts and bright, vibrant colour everywhere. The blossoms on the flowers – the shocking pinks and bright yellows of bougainvillaea, orchids and frangipani, the colour reflected from the iridescent shimmer of fish scales and from the brilliant flapping wings of native birds, which inspired the bold paintings of artist Paul Gauguin. And yet, seeing the photos, the movies and the paintings is nothing compared to the real thing.

The islands of the South Pacific are as exotic as they are distant. Their names are synonymous with legend and mystery – Tahiti, Fiji, Vatulele, Bora Bora, New Caledonia, Samoa, the Solomon and Cook Islands, Easter Island and Tonga. All have the same ingredients – beaches, lagoons, palm trees, wonderful reefs full of dazzling sea life – and yet each one is as different from the rest as it is possible to be. Some are volcanic and dramatic, with high peaks and spectacular waterfalls; others are gentler with little more than a beach, a hotel and a reef; while incredible places such as Easter Island, with its great stone statues, are enigmatic and mysterious. What adds to the desirability and magic of this part of the world is its inaccessibility – the islands are thousands of miles from anywhere. To fly from Europe to even the nearest one – Fiji – will take twenty-five hours without a stopover, which is why many travellers build into their itinerary other places to visit *en route* to the South Pacific – the Far East or Australia and New Zealand to the west, or Los Angeles to the east. (In fact, four cast members chose to break their journey home – one with a stopover in New Zealand and three with a night in LA.)

For many travellers, visiting this part of the world is a once-in-a-lifetime experience, which is why they take extra time to research and plan where they'll go. Fiji is one of the most accessible of the exotic locations, and even though it is known by the one name it is in fact a collection of 330 islands. It is also the most developed of the South Pacific regions, with hotels and lodges to suit all needs and pockets. The place is stunning, and the people outgoing and friendly.

On the other hand, Easter Island, or Rapa Nui to give it its native name, is one of the most remote spots a tourist can visit – 3,700 kilometres from the Chilean coast. It has been a Chilean territory since the late nineteenth century, and its earliest links are believed to have been with South America; it was these possible trade links that Thor Heyerdahl set out to investigate with his famous *Kon-Tiki* expedition in the 1950s. Because of its isolated location, it is one of the least-visited islands in the world. Most people come to see the mysterious statues and other archaeological remains, although the diving there is also spectacular.

The Cook Islands – forever linked with the captains Bligh, Goodenough and, of course, Cook himself – are laid-back and fun, with locals who enjoy singing and dancing more than almost anything else. There are fifteen islands scattered over more than

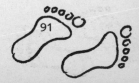

two million square kilometres of ocean, so just getting from one to another is a voyage of discovery.

Vatulele is one of the most exclusive (and expensive) places on earth. A tiny island resort with just seventeen bures (little grass huts of astonishing luxury), it has some of the best scuba diving in the whole region, with twenty-two dive sites all within a fifteen-minute boat ride from the resort. Inland jungle hikes lead to archaeological sites thousands of years old. A place to visit once you've won the Lottery!

Tahiti and its surrounding islands – otherwise known as French Polynesia – is where Paul Gauguin came to paint and lost his heart. Beautiful, exotic and sophisticated, this group of islands, which includes Bora Bora and Moorea, takes up an area larger than Western Europe but receives fewer visitors in a year than Hawaii does in ten days. If you want peace and quiet, you don't need to look anywhere else. Obviously, with all that French influence, the food is fantastic. Everyone who stays on Tahiti (also dubbed the Island of Love), should try to visit Bora Bora, which is regarded as the most beautiful of all the islands, due to its combination of volcanic peaks, lush tropical greenery and a perfect lagoon.

And then there's Tonga, where our cast stayed. Altogether, there are 170 islands in the archipelago, most of them unin-habited, like Nuku. The majority of the locals live on the main island of Tongatapu and this is where the cast landed and spent their first few days getting acclimatized to paradise. This little kingdom has the international date line running right through it, and it is the first place to welcome the new day each morning. The locals are gentle and proud of both their royal family and their history – they are the only South Pacific country that has never been colonized by any foreign power, and the place has been populated since 1100 BC. Much less developed than many other South Pacific islands, Tonga caters for travellers who want simple hotels and lodges rather than the grand and the glitzy. But it is the easiest of all to fall in love with. The diving is spectacularly good (as, of course, is the snorkelling) and the sea life is amazing. It's also one of the few places where, from June to November, you can see the humpback whale when it comes to these waters to mate. Dolphins, sharks, barracuda and many smaller brightly coloured fish as well as some spectacular coral can all be seen within just a few feet of the water's surface. Once the *Shipwrecked* cast summoned up the courage to get out to the reef around Nuku, they could barely stay away from it, as a whole new world was opened up to them. So important are these dive sites that Tonga has five national marine parks and reserves scattered throughout its waters, as well as two land parks.

For any visitor, the islands of the South Pacific imprint themselves firmly on the mind and the memory. And in spite of their deprivations, rows and spats, every single member of the *Shipwrecked* cast said that the island itself was the best thing about their sojourn. What more could any traveller want?

WEEK 3

Monday *Rats in the vegetable garden*

Tuesday *Beautiful man Beach still going*

Wednesday *Wash-day*

Thursday *Victoria leaving*

Friday *Rice and vegetables*

Saturday *Aussie girls want to go home*

Sunday *Rice getting really boring now*

Gradually, everybody began to settle into a routine and grow more comfortable with their surroundings – and naturally, there were good bits as well as hardships. But as they began to relax into themselves, and no longer felt that they had to produce a persona each day, their real characters began to emerge. Naturally, attachments and alliances also formed. Blough, Andy and Kevin became great friends and were invariably together. Although each of them got on equally well with Tim, Jody and Tony, they definitely had a special bond. Jody and Tim had a lot in common, as both are designers, while Tony and Jody also hit it off right from the start. Jody was Tony's great protector and defender, or 'Tony's little henchman', according to Lucy M. Jody also formed an attachment to Larissa and they were often seen strolling on the beach together or curled up in one of the hammocks. Stuart was everybody's favourite guy, but spent most of his time with the girls – particularly Lisa, Emma-Rosa, Lucy T and Samara. Tim also developed a great friendship with and respect for Stuart: 'He's a cracker of a bloke, he's lovely and he's given a lot of people inspiration, and enlightened a few people's minds about gay people. A couple of the lads, I know, were worrying about what to expect, but he's been brilliant with everyone. He's open and will talk to anyone.' Beth developed a great friendship with Jo and Tim – or Timmy Ra as she dubbed him – while the Aussies in general stuck together, although they all got on particularly well with Lucy M. Just as the waves that lap the island's coastline form bonds and disperse, so the friendships and alliances among the cast changed and changed about. Some may last forever, others for just the short time they had together, but every one would have a lasting effect on the Shipwrecked Seventeen.

Within days of meeting, the cast were already trying to categorize each other into recognizable types. Lucy M was the

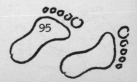

Tim

Best:

Coral reef/swimming.

Seeing Nuku for the first time.

Climbing trees.

Stars at night.

Going to the mainland (staying with Ernie).

Worst:

Long-drop.

Rainy days.

Washing pants.

Going hungry.

People leaving.

first to get to the nub of each character, describing Jo as the glamorous one, Tony as the posh one, Victoria as the alternative one and Jody as Mr Buildingman!

After just a few days, Tim was captivated by Lisa, calling her 'a cracking girl, capable of being a really good leader'. He quickly became matey with her, Beth and Jo who is, he says, the best-looking girl on the island – and he felt sure that that all the lads agreed with him. Lucy T's strong opinions and good nature enabled her to categorize her fellow shipwreckees with ease. She felt Jody was a fab leader, although she also thought he had scary eyes! D seemed a bit bossy, and she liked Emma-Rosa, apart from her obsessive desire to have everything colour co-ordinated. Samara, she decided, got a bit too giggly around the boys and Larissa was fine, except that she whined a lot. Blough occasionally scared her because he is so big, and Vic seemed blunt but sweet. Tim, on the other hand, she found funny and caring – a view shared by many of the female castaways.

In general, after three weeks Nuku was a small and happy

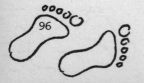

⬆

The girls – (back row, l-r) Lucy M, Emma-Rosa, Jo, Samara, Beth, Lisa;
(front row) Larissa, Victoria and Lucy T.

The boys – (l-r) Stuart, Tim, Andy, Jody, Kevin, Dharma, Tony and Blough.

⬇

Life on the island of Nuku certainly had its ups…

…and downs.

⊕
Tony, Jody and Stuart
in the *Shipwrecked*
kitchen.

The camp – the reality
of desert island life
soon began to sink in.
⊕

Wash-day in paradise.

Blough demonstrates
his personal survival
technique.

All work and no play...Andy chopping coconuts.

Jo finds peace and tranquility in a room of her own.

⊕

Tim works up an appetite.

Rice again – Lucy M and Stuart enjoying their rations.

⊕

The moment of truth as the *Victoria* takes to the waves…

…Captured on film by the ever-present cameras.

Scaring away the girls from the Beautiful Man Beach.

The *Shipwrecked* seventeen.

island with just the occasional outburst of temper and frustration. The whole fiasco between Tony and Lucy M had a very demoralizing effect on the others for a few days, with everyone watching to see if a second spat would take place, while the two pro-tagonists studiously ignored each other. Slowly the business of day-to-day living took over again.

Early on, Larissa com-plained about the fact that everybody was bothering her about what was going on between Jody and herself. She protested that they were just good friends – after all, she had a boyfriend back home – and denied that anything would happen. A few days later, although she had spent a lot of time wrapped around Jody, she moaned about the fact that he tried to kiss her: 'The earth did not move for me and I would rather he didn't try it again.'

'I was totally **shocked** by such behaviour.'
Jo

But in spite of the groupings and pairings, three people stood apart, including Jo, who although she was popular and ostensibly great friends with Samara, Lucy T, Beth and Stuart, is also a very private and self-contained creature. She kept her own counsel and yet when she had something to say, she did so with remarkable articulacy and force. Jo was quick to speak her mind, especially when people did not live up to her high expectations of them. She was disappointed in the way the Aussies reacted to the lads' banter, and took it as a sign of immaturity. When Lucy M observed that Jo taking tea to the boys building the shelter was prehistoric, Jo treated the comment with disdain.

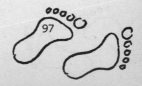

And she was particularly acidic when Lisa and Larissa confessed that they had been stealing food. When Jo first discovered that the theft had taken place, and the identity of the perpetrators, she asked the week's leader, Andy, to call a meeting so that the offenders could confess – which they did, inevitably. They were also joined by Lucy M, who revealed a few misdemeanours of her own. None of this cut any ice with Jo: 'It caused such tension in the camp and it was all caused by people I trusted. In the end, I know they only owned up because they had been rumbled, and that made me even angrier. At least Lucy M admitted that she didn't regret her actions and would do it again if she could. But still, they have all fallen in my estimation.' In spite of such harsh criticism, Jo continued to weave, sew, give good counsel and sunbathe, keeping most of her thoughts to herself.

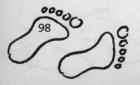

'I just can't cope with people in general.'
victoria

Victoria, on the other hand, had been angst-ridden from the word go and felt completely isolated from the group. As early as the first week, she was racked with doubts, both about her suitability for the task ahead of her and about her desire to be on the island. On day four she admitted that she felt disconnected from the rest of the group: 'Each day I just feel worse and worse and I don't know why. It is so stupid and I feel so guilty about being unhappy in this really beautiful place. I haven't felt this miserable since I was at school, and I hated that. I don't hate this. It is made even worse by the fact that I tried so hard to get here, but every day I want more and more to go home.' But, she emphasized, she was determined to stick it out.

However, the next day her feelings had not improved. 'It's my own fault, I know that. It's my fault that I can't relate to people who know where they are going. I have no set way of life. I just want to listen to music.' And she continued to beat herself up over her so-called attitude problem: 'I thought I was more mature and now I find I can't cope being outside my own environment. I really want to be back there where it's safe and where it's OK not to have a job or go to uni. I want to go home so much, but I won't – I'm going to stick this out.' Victoria clearly felt that her problems were all to do with her own mentality. She claimed to like everybody, but... 'they make me feel so bad about myself, as if I could never accomplish anything. I'm sure I would be alright if I just had some punk.'

Victoria confessed to Blough that she would have been absolutely fine if she could have had some beer and listened to the Dead Kennedys. She also told him that she felt much more able to talk to the hut-cam than to anybody in the group (although she had initially ridiculed the idea), and even gave the camera, her confessor, a name – George. 'I don't even get on well with people at home,' she admitted. 'I don't trust people. But here you have to trust people. I don't know why I thought I could cope with this or how I could get along with a bunch of strangers.' She was particularly upset with herself over her own unhappiness as she felt that the life on the island was everything that she had thought she wanted.

To her credit, throughout her misery Victoria analyzed why she is the way she is and what, if anything, she could do about it. On another occasion, she told George that she thought her problem was to do with the fact that she found it difficult to be

herself away from her own scene. But even though she was incredibly homesick, she vowed again to carry on.

Many of the group realized that Victoria was unhappy and thinking of leaving, and they were kind and supportive to her. At one point she was so sad that the rest of the group decided to have a party – a punk party – to cheer her up. The girls spent hours on their wardrobe and Samara asked Vic to help her dye her hair pink, while others appeared in torn fishnets, ripped jumpers and vibrant make-up. Jo even made up the boys, in bright blues and pinks. It was also time for another luxury from the mainland, and in honour of their youngest and unhappiest member, the cast voted for chocolate. Vic was thrilled and swore to renew her efforts to stay.

Most of the cast felt that if Vic was really so unhappy then she should have gone home, although they didn't want to lose her. Lucy M knew that if she were that miserable she would really want to go back and told the other Lucy that most of the time she wanted to leave too, because she was feeling very homesick. 'I hope Vic doesn't go,' she commented, 'because she's a really nice girl. But if she stays here for the whole ten weeks being this miserable, it could really affect her badly when she eventually goes home.' Ever the pragmatist, Lucy T knew how dependent Vic was on her tobacco, and in her usual forthright fashion told the others, 'If she runs out of tobacco it will be a nightmare and I don't want to be here for weeks with someone who is a complete nightmare.'

However, despite the group's warm feelings towards her, Vic's sense of alienation grew. On the beach with Samara, Emma, Jo and Beth, she was completely fazed by what she termed their 'girliness': 'There are so many girls here. It's hair, it's face, it's clipping toenails, tanning and girls galore, and I know nothing about it.' One evening, talking to the lads and Lucy T, it suddenly dawned on Vic that they all had problems understanding her problem: 'So perhaps that's why I'm so unhappy, because these people have made me realize that I don't know what I am doing with my life.'

But there was no peace for poor Vic's confused mind until one morning she headed straight for George and told the hut-cam that during the night she had what alcoholics call a moment of clarity. 'I have finally decided that I want to stay. There are only eight weeks left; surely I can [stick it for that long]. Even if I don't like it sometimes, even if I run out of tobacco, which is bound to happen in the next week. Everyone is homesick, it's not just me. I would hate to miss out on the boat and plane journey home with everyone – knowing that we did it, that we survived.' But, prophetically, she turned back to face the camera before leaving the hut to comment, 'Having said all of that, I'll probably be back here tomorrow saying I want to go home. Aaaaah!'

In-between moments of real misery, Vic did make a conscious effort to be positive and to join in with the others. The fact that she wasn't very good at all the physical stuff that needed doing – building, weaving, cooking and fishing – also got her down, but she was always ready to lend a hand. She chided herself for thinking she hadn't fitted in and pointed out to herself how well the Australians had done so, despite the fact that they had all come from a very different background to that of the Brits. And while she was mostly very pro the Aussies, and told Kevin off really severely for what she described as his 'rude and oafish' behaviour towards them, she did criticize the girls quite strongly for misunderstanding the British sense of humour. 'Poor Tony came out of the whole affair quite badly and he is very upset about it. Lucy's argument that he was the main protagonist is based on sod all and she is responsible for winding the girls up... I have no idea why she is doing it.'

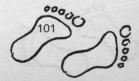

Victoria

Best:
Sunsets.

Sleeping on the beach.

The millions of stars.

Isolation from the world.

Each person I met.

Worst:
The whole 'school trip' feel about it all.

Cameras!

Feeling I couldn't be myself.

Ignorance from everyone (including me) about each others beliefs/interests.

Saying goodbye to paradise.

In retaliation, Vic told Lisa, who was leader at the time, that Lucy had been stealing from the crew's camp. 'I'd known for a time that she had been stealing chocolate and cokes and I felt that it might affect our own luxury items and that they might get stopped or changed. She also let other people take the blame, which is not good or honest, and although I felt bad about telling on her, I also did it to put her accusations against Tony in perspective.'

Sadly, in spite of such public spiritedness and occasional moments of fun and serenity, in the third week Vic admitted defeat, and told Lisa that she wanted to leave the island. However, leaving paradise was never going to be simple. In the island's constitution, which each member had to sign and accept before leaving home (see pages 28–31), very stringent rules were laid down. If anyone wanted to leave, or felt they

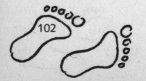

wanted to nominate someone else to go, they had first to get the permission of the production team and then get a minimum of fourteen votes from their peers. The only compassionate grounds on which people were allowed to leave the island were health problems, bad news from home – which would be relayed by the production crew – or mental distress. And everyone was made fully aware that boredom did not constitute 'mental distress'. While most people were fond of Vic and really did not want her to leave so soon, in the end they all recognized her extreme unhappiness and gave her their votes, followed by a goodbye party.

'You spend so much time on this island suppressing your emotions.'

Stuart

Given that they had given her both their permission and blessing, Vic's leaving had a profound effect on the group – for in spite of their perkiness and brightness most of them had suffered severe bouts of homesickness themselves. Of course, they missed their creature comforts, but what depressed them more than anything was not being near family and friends. Most of these feelings had been kept at bay through a mixture of bravado and the extraordinariness of their surroundings, but scratch the surface and all that longing was right there. Some of the cast coped by telling each other of their loneliness, others by going alone late at night to the hut-cam and leaving messages for their friends, lovers and families so that eventually, when the series was shown, those at home would know that they had not been forgotten. Some, Beth for instance, smuggled in letters to

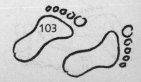

comfort themselves: 'I sneaked in three letters from my mum and opened them at various times throughout the ten weeks. I didn't always leave them until the days she told me to open them – they were all read much sooner.' But despite the fact that she had some comfort from home Beth, like many of the others, was deeply affected by Vic's departure. 'It was better for her, but we all missed her, we missed the way she looked and her little mad stories – suddenly we weren't complete.' Stuart, always the liveliest one, wandered off across the island on his own and wept bitterly. 'I cried not because I was going to miss her that much, but for myself. I began to realize that I wanted to go home too, and that's what upset me.' Even action man Jody was forced to admit that if he didn't keep himself busy all the time he would be thinking of home. 'It was so strange watching her leave, because it made it all seem so easy and I suddenly realized that there would be no shame attached to wanting to leave, which was very tempting. But then I thought what she was missing out on.'

And Vic's departure made Jo even more introspective, although she admitted a few days before Vic left that she really couldn't wait for her to go, 'so that my homesickness could go with her. Her leaving made me think so much of home but I keep telling myself that there's only another seven weeks to go. I am glad for her sake she is gone. She was so unhappy and I respect her for following her heart. But part of me thinks that she will regret it in the long term.'

Even though she left them so early in their adventure, Vic was often talked about and much missed. Day by day they wondered how she was doing and whether she was any happier. To keep her memory alive, Jody named the group's canoe Victoria. Once it was repaired and made seaworthy he carved her name into it, while on their very last week, feeling more than

de-mob happy and bored with having leaders, they all decided that the absent Vic would be their leader for that final week.

With the benefit of hindsight, Vic was able to put her feelings about being shipwrecked into perspective. 'I really miss them all,' she admitted once she had got home. 'They were wonderful and I could have lived on the island for ever but I couldn't cope with the idea of being a character in a TV programme… I couldn't cope with the intrusiveness of the camera and felt I had to be careful and watch what I said all the time. It was all my fault and I still feel guilty about taking up a place that someone else would have really loved.'

To help to blow the blues away, Stuart began to organize and rehearse the opening ceremony of the island Olympics, an idea that D came up with, inspired by the Olympics 2000 in Sydney. It was also a way for D to preserve his sanity and to stay the course – but could he do so among all these Brits?

WEEK 4

Monday *Row between Aussie girls and lads made up*

Tuesday *Rice and cabbage again*

Wednesday *Rehearsals begin for Olympics*

Thursday *Skived off to beach - bored with work*

Friday *Start fishing*

Saturday *D gone missing*

Sunday *Swam to reef — sharks!*

The cast tried to settle down after Vic's departure, but even though sixteen of them were left, the whole group dynamic had changed. Everyone was beginning to question whether they really knew anybody on the island, and whether it was true friendship or simply expediency that was making them form their alliances.

Lisa confessed in her diary that such thoughts kept her awake at night: 'I started to think how vulnerable we are. All of us are here on display in so many ways, our personalities are under the microscope and we have left ourselves open to judgement. Is it possible to like someone when you have seen them under such raw [circumstances] as we are living [under]? It is hard for people to see us as likeable... but I found myself looking at myself from many different angles and I found that I do like my-self... and the judgment of others is superfluous.' Meanwhile, Larissa and Jody pondered the idea that friendships formed in unusual situations such as theirs rarely last, because they're born out of necessity.

'It's so strange to think that people will watch us and form opinions.'
Lisa

Slowly, each castaway was becoming forced to rely their own strengths and resources. But at the same time they were discovering new things about themselves and each other. Even Tim, who normally came across as happy and carefree, was beginning to feel the strain. 'I can't believe some of the things people are talking about,' he groaned. 'It's mostly sex and food. I have thought this before... I felt I shouldn't

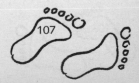

comment on the fact that there is no intellectual stimulation here, but it is now really getting to me. I have to keep reminding myself why I am here. I thought I might become a different, stronger person and learn something different about myself – well it hasn't happened yet. Maybe it will when I get back!' But there's always an up side where Tim is concerned, and he looked to Blough whenever he felt a little low. 'I have bonded with him quite well and we do have good conversations,' he reflected. 'Every time I look at him I grin, especially when he is floating belly up in the sea – you know he is having a good time, and you can't help but enjoy him as well.'

'I have a deep craving for a decent conversation.'
Tim

Andy was concerned that the atmosphere was still a bit fake and that people were afraid to be themselves. 'The fact that we have been OK so far is a credit to us, but it's strange because no one here is similar to my friends at home. It's a completely different environment for me, and not one I'm used to, but I expect it's the same for everyone else, which is why we're still pretty much walking on eggshells. It will be interesting to see if people change and if they start to show their true colours'. In a more introspective mood, he wondered why some people had come to the island at all, but admitted that the most exciting prospect for them was that they had been given a chance that was not normally granted to people and that they should treasure it. Some people had told Andy that they wanted to change their lives, but he had already made a decision to change when he accepted the challenge to come to Nuku.

'For ten years all I ever thought about was football, there was nothing else. I just wanted to be a professional footballer, hit the big time and do really well. But the moment I decided to come here I realized that maybe there is more to life than football. I

Andy

Best:
One night I went out in the middle of the night and the sky was lit up with stars that shone brighter than a full moon.

The most amazing sunsets I have ever seen, or, I'm sure, will ever see.

The freedom – I had no real responsibility or problems on my mind, everything I did was for the moment, without having to worry about long-term repercussions. There were times when I was totally at peace with myself.

The fact that I am now a connoisseur of coconuts.

I was the coconut-finder general. I had a knack of finding the tastiest, juiciest, sexiest coconuts in the South Pacific.

I made some great friends on the island, people that I would have never met if I hadn't had the opportunity to go. Being around the same people twenty-four-seven for ten weeks really makes you bond with each other, and you get genuinely close. I've now got friends all over the place and they are all completely different. Cast and crew.

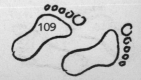

Worst:

To have a cup of tea I had to trek through the woods to hack down and collect dry wood to start a fire to boil the water. It took about half an hour. When I had eventually boiled the water, the tea that we had was the worst tea in the world ever! Which is why I got rid of a box of two hundred in the time capsule.

Walking barefoot on the beach and stepping on sharp coral washed up on the shore.

When cooking and standing over the fire, having really hot smoke blowing into my eyes

which made them sting, made me go temporarily blind and made my eyes go redder than Tim's nose!

Continually hacking into parts of my body, particularly my hands, with machetes, leathermen, Swiss army knives and chopping knives – I've got the scars to prove it. I used to have such beautiful hands!

Being so far away from my loved ones and not even being able to talk to them or keep in touch to tell them all of the things I had been doing, and let them know how I was feeling.

told myself that I had given the last ten years to the game, so the next ten weeks is for me.'

It took Andy a little time to get a handle on other people; he didn't realize that they may not have had the same interests or sense of humour as him. For instance, he thought initially that he and Samara were getting on really well. Then one day it dawned on him that he had upset her a couple of times. 'I was joking, but she took [my comments] seriously,' he recalled.

'I thought at twenty-three she would be more mature, but she is acting like a sixteen-year-old. She's really sensitive, and she thinks I've picked on her. But I can't suddenly change into somebody else. I'm me, and this is the way I am.'

The food situation hadn't improved by the fourth week, and everybody was getting fed up and ratty. Tim, normally quiet and accepting, confessed that he was feeling hungrier than he had ever felt in his life. The vegetable garden provided cabbage, beetroot, lettuces and tomatoes, which the group mixed with rice to form their staple meal. They needed to get more fish and no matter how hard the guys tried – it was mainly Jody, Tony, Tim and Kev who fished – they rarely found enough. They returned from one fishing expedition with three large fish and a handful of small ones, but another day Jody and Tony went out three times and caught nothing. The guys knew that in order to increase their fish intake they had to fish farther out on the reef, and for that they needed the boat.

'I am so hungry, I'd be happy to eat my own buttock.'
Tim

The canoe was found on the island by the camera crew before the cast arrived – it had been abandoned by a local fisherman. However, it was still in fairly good shape so, for the purposes of the programme, they needed to bash it about a bit; now the cast had to make it seaworthy again. Jody was volunteered for the job, with some extra help from D, Tony and Tim, who's the real master craftsman on the island. This caused an outburst from Kevin, who was desperate to do something for the group

that he could be proud of. 'I told Tony when he was leader in the first week that I would like to have a go at the boat,' he revealed, 'but he said we had to concentrate on the shelter first. By the time we got round to the boat it was suddenly all being done by Jody. It's always Jody this and Jody that – it's not his fault I know, he's a really lovely guy. I really love him, but I would really like to do something for the group.'

But life had to go on while Jody was working on the boat and trying to find a tree with the right sort of resin to fill the holes in it. The guys spent their time fishing and swimming. For Jody, swimming was a personal triumph. 'I had a real phobia about swimming out of my depth before going to Nuku. I was terrified of sea water, because I got stung by a jellyfish when I was a child. But within weeks it had gone. I had conquered the fear.'

In their search for fish they went further and further out to the reef, where every single one of them fell in love with the life under the sea. One day, on their return, they came across a shark about eight feet long, which completely mesmerized them. Jody went straight towards it, even though he was terrified: 'I had to do it. I had to say I had swum with a shark,' he explained later. And then another smaller one, a leopard shark, came along. Kevin was beside himself with joy: 'I couldn't believe what I was seeing. The big one was so beautiful.' The minute the lads brought their fish back – hanging around in the open seas with a load of dead fish and two live sharks suddenly seemed to be a bad idea – Kevin got straight back into the water and headed off on a shark hunt to see if they were still there. Such revelatory moments would often occur to individual cast members out of the blue, and reinforce their determination to stick it out on the island. One such moment happened to Kevin after a hard day's fishing. 'I was swimming back having caught very little all day and I was cold and tired. Suddenly I stopped and looked at the island and realized that it

Kevin

Best:

The sun – both with its sunsets and sunrises – made the ten weeks.

The sea – it was so clear and blue, and it was really beautiful to see all the life there as well.

The shark – I've never seen one before, but I wasn't scared for some reason, I just wanted to swim with it.

Getting to the mainland – me, Andy and Tim set off on an adventure, and this was probably my favourite few days.

Seeing the island – when we first saw the island from a distance it was like a scene from a movie. We couldn't have wished for a better place.

Worst:

Mosquitoes and flies – these were rife on the island and woke me up every morning.

Long-drop – although I found this really amusing, it was disgusting. Sixteen other people's shit stacked up with flies was horrible.

The rain – although it was sometimes refreshing, there just wasn't a lot to do.

The rum – nearly having my mainland trip taken from me.

Leaving – very mixed emotions.

was home and I belonged there. It was a good feeling. I know the place and the people took a lot of getting used to, but I think that when we get back everything will be fine for the first week [and]

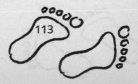

after that we will want to come back to Nuku.'

However, by now lone Australian male D, like Victoria before him, was starting to feel more and more isolated. Sure, he helped with the building and fishing, he climbed for coconuts and found papaya, but that was as far as his involvement went. He mixed mainly with the Australian girls and Lucy M, whom he felt was different to the other members of the group, as they – the Australians – were different. Normally he just wandered off around the island and seethed to himself, but every so often he hit the confessional hut to really let off steam. At one stage, quite early on in the proceedings, he unloaded a lot of frustration over his fellow castaways: 'I feel as if I have been shipwrecked with the most boring people in the world – they are completely unadventurous. No one even wants to climb a coconut tree because they have no confidence in their own abilities. The most adventurous thing any of them do is get up in the morning and go get a tan.' From the outset, D complained about what he perceived as the Brits' laziness. However, there was one exception to his blanket condemnation of the British castaways: Vic. 'She was one of the nicest people here,' he commented, 'and I really hoped she wouldn't go. But in the end her happiness was more important.'

Yet despite his own unhappiness, D had his admirers. While several of the group thought him dry and stand-offish, they all recognized that he was one of the hardest workers. However, they were sad that he couldn't loosen up and stop taking everything far too seriously. Especially the Island Olympics. They were D's idea and he pushed the idea forward from the minute he met up with the group in Tonga. Now the Brits were quite keen for a bit of fun and a bit of sport, but D was a man with a mission. Jody summed up the differences in their approach to the idea when he pointed out that, more than anything, the Olympics should be a 'good laugh'. D wanted to include a coconut climb as part of the games, although that idea was vetoed by the girls, who felt that it was too dangerous. It got to the stage at which D felt that everything he suggested had to be modified.

'It's just not working for me here,' he moaned at one point. 'I thought it would be more survival than social experiment, but there are too many differences. I don't want to deal with all these little minor arguments any more. I would rather take away half the rations and half the people. If we didn't have rice to eat every night it would break a lot of people very quickly. Most of them haven't even opened a coconut,. There's plenty of food around and they haven't even been into the forest to look for papaws. I do find it very hard to deal with the Britishness of such a large group. I want to escape from it and live for myself a bit more and enjoy the place. And what really annoys me is that I can guarantee that at least half the people haven't even been to explore the reef. I'm sure half of them haven't been around the island more than once.'

And so it continued – one seriously disgruntled guy against the world. But even D knew that the situation couldn't go on. Instead, he talked himself into a shift in attitude and woke up one morning with the power of positive thinking motivating him to rise above the situation. 'Most people here I can't stand to live with,' he confessed. 'I am very different from them, but I have to accept that they are not going to change and neither am I, so we must go our separate

'I don't care who leaves; everyone can go except me, I'll stick it out.'
Stuart

ways for the rest of the stay.' He confessed that he had a plan to go and live on Fukave on his own, but had discovered this was not feasible and so would have to put up with the others for the duration. He resolved to steer clear of certain cast members, although he had now begun to warm to some of the others. 'Lucy T I find really hard. She's loud and obnoxious and I don't want anything to do with her. Beth has been unwilling to meet me halfway, so I don't care about her anymore. Emma is a nice girl but a bit of a power tripper, while Lisa is the strongest one here and I'm glad she's here.'

Apart from Tony, whom he liked and respected, D believed that all the other guys were engaged in a popularity contest – and that was something he was not prepared to join in with. He admitted that he was on the island for himself rather than the group, and that he had learnt some valuable lessons about himself. He then wondered whether he should ask the Aussie girls to propose him as leader. 'I know who the next leaders will be: Tim, Emma, Kevin – all popularity votes. However, I think it would be interesting and funny to see who would vote for me – that would make all sorts of things clearer.' In the end, though, he decided not to pursue the leadership cause!

What D did decide to do, though, was to move out and set up his own camp to get away from the others, to pursue a sense of isolation and to get a bit of peace and quiet. One day, while walking around the island, he found a great site that couldn't be seen from the beach. He began to plan how to build a camp and how to secure rations. 'I just want to do my own thing, I can't be free enough in my mind with sixteen other people screaming and yelling in their English way. We're just totally different – we can get on, but it's not what I'm here for.' The more he ruminated, the clearer D's plan became, but he decided to put the move off until after the Olympics, in case it rocked the boat.

FOOD...

More than any other single topic, food featured at the top of every conversation and wish list of the Nuku castaways. At the beginning of their stay they were provided with a list of available foodstuffs from which they had to order weekly rations. The list included:

> twenty kilos of rice
> twenty tins of vegetables
> thirty tins of meat – mostly corned beef
> twenty tins of fish – a mix of mackerel, sardines
> thirty kilos of local fresh vegetables
> twenty kilos of local fresh fruit

plus biscuits, tea bags, coffee, sugar, cabin bread, salt and powdered milk, not to mention nine bottles of rum. The cast were also allowed vitamin C in the form of limes – all those history lessons about scurvy-stricken sailors obviously didn't go to waste – and a multi-vitamin tablet every day.

Each week they were given a choice of three luxuries, from which they were allowed to choose one. And while the list included important elements such as nails, oars and a map, it also offered ice cream, chickens and chocolate – all of which were voted for at one time or another.

The rest of their food they had to forage for, mostly from the sea, but a large garden of salad and other vegetables had been planted for them. However, even though the latter was ready for consumption by week one, they really didn't get stuck into

it until week three – mostly because they weren't sure what some of the plants were. But once they had sussed the sweet potatoes, the lettuces and beetroot, their main problem was keeping it watered and safe from the rats, which found the potatoes just too tempting.

To begin with, the cast's main problem was how to water the garden, as not too many of them had any knowledge of horticulture. However, they knew that sea water was not the best thing for the job because the salt in it would kill the crops. During an exploratory trawl across the island one day, a group of them came across an old rainwater barrel, which they adapted for use in the garden. Fortunately, there were enough tropical rainstorms during their stay on the island to keep it well topped up. Beth became the self-appointed gardener and tended the plants with great care.

But none of this alleviated the endless complaints and whines of hunger, not to mention the lack of choice. Lucy M was the most philosophical about the rations. 'I don't think I expected much,' she reflected later. 'We did know we were going to a desert island, so I wasn't expecting great things. Anyway, I'm a vegetarian and seemed to live on rice and beetroot.'

Larissa, who claimed she was used to six meals a day, found both the amounts of food and the meagre choice the worst things about being on Nuku. She also thought that lack of food was having a terrible effect on people's psyches, which is why she complained about some of the boys behaving like twelve year-olds. She even thought at one stage she might be suffering from malnutrition – though others put that down to her desire to be the centre of attention.

But after the first three weeks, the cast gradually began to accept the concept of rations, the limitations of what was available to eat and how they could survive without all the pizzas, pastas

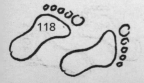

and takeaways that they had left at home. Sometimes, they would masochistically describe in detail their favourite roast dinners, lingering over the best way to cook the roast potatoes and debate whether they were better with or without gravy! And all of this while the temperature was well above thirty degrees Celsius. But even shipwreckees can dream, and these castaways at least had the option to request chocolate and ice cream as luxuries.

Having forsworn the idea of pigs for the pork, it took the cast a while to recover from the shock of seeing blood spilt during Ernie's pig butchering demonstration, and they were still pretty squeamish when it came to the chickens. The first lot were killed most efficiently by Blough, but the rest of the lads were not too enamoured at the thought of plucking and drawing the birds, even though they eventually went through with the tasks.

A few weeks later, when it was time for the second onslaught on the chickens, the girls felt a little braver and decided that they should be the ones to kill them this time. Unable to face the idea of wringing their necks, Larissa decided they should chop the chickens' heads off and the group duly trooped down to the beach to watch the event. Unfortunately, the first chop missed, terrifying both the poor bird and Larissa! After that, the girls decided that killing was best left to the boys, as was most of the fishing – a decision Jo had made right at the very beginning. Much to the horror of the Aussie girls and Lucy M, she had explained that boys were better at building, fishing and killing, while girls could weave, cook and sew!

Two of the most difficult jobs on the entire island were to do with food and rations. Lisa and Emma-Rosa were put in charge of rations and keeping an eye on how food was distributed. Both girls found this quite stressful, particularly when everyone started nicking biscuits! They had devised a scheme whereby everyone was allowed two crackers for each meal. However, this quickly

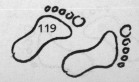

fell into disarray because some people wanted more for breakfast and none later on, while others wanted their daily rations in the morning so that they could eke out snacks throughout the day. Before long, everyone was trading their food – someone who didn't take sugar would swap their spoonfuls for extra crackers or coffee, while others would leave it in the pot but believe that entitled them to an extra helping of fruit or veg at dinner. Andy even traded his chocolate to whoever would take his turn at washing up! Before long, squabbles arose about who was eating what, who was taking the last of the powdered milk and why the cooks were giving themselves larger helpings at meal times – just like an everyday student flatshare...

Many took it in turns to do the cooking, including Andy and Blough, Stuart, Lisa and Emma-Rosa, and because everything was so bland, they had to try hard to be inventive. Emma-Rosa had used her initiative and brought a box of spices to the island as one of her luxury items. She guarded them carefully, saving many of them for special celebrations, such as birthdays. Or, indeed, for the day she went fishing with Tony and Jody and, with beginner's luck, they caught an octopus. The three of them chopped it up and Emma-Rosa fried it with chilli – 'very tasty, if a bit chewy,' she decided. In fact, culinary war almost broke out at one stage, with Andy and Emma-Rosa claiming to be the best chefs, which left Lisa, who fancied herself as a really good cook, fuming.

The sea looked enticing and the reef was full of the most glorious fish, but catching them wasn't as easy as everybody had thought at first. It took a number of fishing trips before anything happened. Nevertheless, it was a great day when Tony, Jody and Kev brought home the first lot towards the end of the first week, even though there were only about six small ones to feed them all! Gradually, the fishing improved, but not before several fruitless expeditions, which led the cast to fall back on their tins of meat or make do with yet more beetroot, cabbage and rice! It became more and more imperative for them to fix their rickety boat, because the only way they were going to catch a sufficient amount was to get farther and farther out to sea. But even when they finally got the handle on catching fresh food, the complaints didn't stop. The whole thing was given a kick-start when the cast were told their rations were going to be cut back about halfway through their stay, leading to even more culinary anxiety and creeping fears of malnutrition.

But one person positively welcomed the news – D. His outward-bound Aussie streak came to the fore with the realization that there might be no food left by the last week or two. 'Of course it's no fun eating rice every night, but some of these people really need to know what being shipwrecked is really like,' he maintained. He was particularly cross with those who hadn't even bothered to explore the island or the reef and who were too idle, as he saw it, to get off their butts and go pick papayas, which were growing wild all over the island.

Emma-Rosa was instantly labelled a food queen when it became known one of her luxuries was a box of spices. So it naturally followed that cooking would be one area of a major contribution from her. At first the food was pretty bland, and all of them knew they would need to be far more inventive if they were to enjoy their island meals. And the real foodies – Lisa, Blough, Andy and Stuart – all chipped in with ideas and recipes, to provide some small surprise for their tastebuds occasionally. Emma-Rosa kept some notes in her diary on the process and also devised a few recipes of her own:

'Lisa and I were put in charge of the rations and became head chefs of Nuku. The thought of cooking for seventeen hungry mouths with our boring rations scared me. We had our assistants, Andy and Stuart, and our main chopper, Blough. I had a little

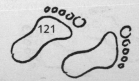

advantage when it came to cooking tasty meals because my luxury item was a bag of spices. I got the nickname Sexy Mama on the island, probably because I was the oldest and cooked a lot. Anyway I shared out my spices and saved the special meals for Lucy T's birthday (Thai Green Curry) and D's birthday (Chinese Hot Curry), and our last meal was Thai Green again.'

Thai Green Curry

Thai green curry paste (half a bag!)
Coconut milk (ten coconuts! Everyone helped collect, hack open and grind. Stuart and I squeezed the flakes to milk.)

Heat this together and add four cups of water. You can add red chillies if it's not spicy enough. We served this with rice, cabbage and sweet potato.

Chinese Hot Curry

Chinese curry paste (half a bag!)
Coconut juice (five coconuts. No grinding, just hack open and pour out the juice)
Dried red chillies (a handful)
Onions (ten)

Melt the paste into the juice. Stir fry the onions and chillies in a little oil and then add to the sauce. Andy and I served this with rice and sweetcorn.

WEEK 5

Monday *Only two fish between all of us*

Tuesday *Everybody starving*

Wednesday *D's camp discovered*

Thursday *More fishing*

Friday *Sick of fish*

Saturday *No more food drops!*

Sunday *Long-drop disgusting and full of flies*

As the Island Olympics progressed, the tension caused by the competition rose among some members of the group. A number of them blamed D. Kev, for instance, thought D had got too short a fuse and had really only tried to bond with the Aussie girls, while Jody thought he was dry and unfriendly. The sporting events got to most people, however, although Jody, Beth and Lucy all were determined not to take them too seriously. Occasionally, therefore, during one of the events they pretended to fall over, or miss a target quite deliberately. At one point, Kev accused Beth of deliberately elbowing Jo to get her disqualified. Eventually, the unwilling three admitted that sabotage was on their minds. Samara was one of the first to get really cross with them – especially after she won the long jump: 'I've suddenly realized that I am quite competitive, so I'm really pleased to have come first.' If Emma and Kev, two of her team-mates, weren't going to take the whole thing seriously, their chances of being overall winners were limited.

At the same time, the boys concocted a scheme to scare the girls – a sort of *Blair Witch* scenario. Every so often, when some of the girls were in earshot, they started talking about hearing voices on different parts of the island – and not voices that any of them recognized. A little later, one of the lads started discussing the prison island, which was just a few miles away on the other side of the reef. Later that night, as Lucy T went to the long-drop, she heard a crashing noise and nearly jumped out of her skin – in fact, it was a coconut falling... or was it? Over the next day or two, other strange things happened – a machete went missing, along with various bits of clothing. The lads, when they believed nobody was listening, or pretended nobody was, started talking about an escaped convict. One of them claimed a fisherman told them about it when they met him over at Fukave, and they surmised that perhaps he had turned

up on Nuku, where there was food and a few foreigners. The girls' anxiety increased when three of the boys swam over to Fukave and found one of Tony's T-shirts there, despite the fact that Tony had been nowhere near that island for days! By this time, Larissa, Samara and Lucy T were totally spooked – so much so, that Lucy refused to go the long-drop after dark. In the end the whole thing fizzled out, mainly because Tim pointed out how unfair it was to make people afraid of where they live.

The rest of the girls had always suspected that it was the boys play-acting, and wanted to retaliate but couldn't come up with a sufficiently convincing idea. The production team had brought a supply of condoms onto the island, and the girls wondered whether they should use them as water bombs and invade the Beautiful

'The Brits are over-cautious and under-confident.'

D

Man Beach. Lisa had some laxatives, and they considered ways of crushing them into the guys' food. Luckily, they decided that not only would that be to too difficult to do secretly, but the long-drop was disgusting enough without adding to its load! In the end, all such ideas were dropped and the group got back into their four teams to continue with the Olympics. Even though his side were winning, D was still confused and contemptuous of the Brits. Firstly, because they vetoed his idea for the opening ceremony – he wanted them all to dance with firesticks, which they felt would be too dangerous, and although they all held

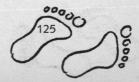

torches, only one was lit. And secondly, because when he voiced the opinion that the relay race should be around the island, it was voted down because most of the others felt it would be too dangerous, as the rocks were very slippery. D was not impressed. 'No wonder we always kick their arses in sporting contests!' he sneered. D's perception of the British attitude fuelled his determination to move away from them all.

His honour was salvaged, however, when his team (Jo, Tim and Lucy M) won the Olympics outright. They were thrilled with the huge carved medals that the crew had commissioned from a local craftsman, and which were presented to them at the end of the events. Wearing their medals with pride, they did a lap of honour, hollering their war cry: 'What are we? Blondes, Aussie and lesbian!'

The other thing the amateur Olympics achieved was to make them all examine the group mentality that taken over on the island. From the outset, they had agreed that any decision that affected them all had to be made by popular vote. They also voted in regular meetings where people could voice their worries,

---

Blough

Best:	Worst:
The reef.	*Wind.*
People.	*Rain.*
The survival element.	*Food.*
Building the Cosa Nostra.	*Smelly clothes.*
The sunsets.	*Lack of privacy.*

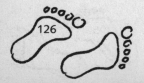

thoughts and criticisms, for it was felt that the democratic principle was the only way in which the island and its inhabitants could work efficiently. Although some began to think the meetings were a waste of time, nobody came up with a viable alternative.

Blough and Jody were the most vociferous about their dislike of too many meetings. 'I'm sick of meetings and votings, sick of the democracy of everything having to be done in meetings,' Jody raged. 'I think people are overly contributing to meetings when the cameras are there. I think we are all having an identity crisis, wondering what our niche is.'

In one of her more introspective moments, Lisa ruminated on the concept of the group mentality versus the individual. 'Back home we would hate to be seen as sheep but here we have pulled together in a real sense of community and group rule is working,' she mused. 'Back home or at school we would rebel against such strictures, but here on our own it's a practical way of living. The people who are getting worked up about too many votes and meetings are doing so for irrelevant reasons, like not wanting to do the washing up. What I really feel and am trying to express is that we are all individuals here and don't need to prove it.'

Jody, on the other hand, felt that there were only two real individuals – 'Lucy M because she is so stubborn and self-righteous and D, who has mentally removed himself from the group.'

At this juncture, Jody had no idea that D was in the process of removing himself from the group physically as well as mentally. Tony was the first to tell him after he had discovered D's shelter, but swore him to secrecy too. But you can't keep too many secrets on a tiny island – people not only stumble across things, they notice changes in behaviour too. And people don't come any shrewder than Lucy M, who noticed that D was

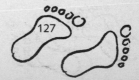

> **'I feel more like a sheep than an individual.'**
> Jody

absenting himself more and more from the group. In the end, she confronted him when they were alone together and demanded to know where he kept disappearing to. He confessed that he had set up a little camp on the other side of the island because he really wasn't having enough fun with the other shipwreckees. He told her it was alright for the Aussie girls because they had each other, but while he liked all the guys, they really had nothing in common with him:

'I'm not doing this to split the camp, I'm just doing it for myself. I don't find the rest of the people adventurous enough. All the other guys don't have to adapt or adjust to a different society – they don't have to, they have each other, the only real shift they have to make is eating rice every day. Because I'm the lone Aussie guy, I do have to make adjustments. When it's one-on-one, like with you, Lucy, I'm very happy, but when it's the whole group having the same conversations all the time, telling the same jokes, I can't cope. I don't want to. The whole thing is a big social experiment when I thought it would be more about survival.'

He then told her that Tony had discovered his camp earlier that day, and although he promised him he wouldn't tell, D wasn't sure whether he could trust him or not. And although D told Lucy that he liked all the other guys, that hadn't always been the case – at the beginning he found them really difficult to tune into. Tony and Jody he got on with and respected

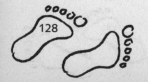

because he saw them as workers like himself, but in general he felt a huge sense of isolation. Deep down, he had been looking for a way out almost since the second week. 'It's really somewhere to sleep so I'm not surrounded by sixteen others,' he confessed. 'I hope the group won't take it the wrong way but they probably will, because I can't see them understanding the reasons why I'm doing it.' The site D chose was perfect, he felt: up on the rocks away from the beach, but 'with great views and a wonderful platform to see the sun rise.'

As time went by, D began to grow to accept most of the rest of the group. The only one he felt he had nothing in common with was Kev, and the person he really clicked with was Lucy M. 'People see her as different,' he commented, 'and us Aussies as different, and that may have something to do with it.'

While D could trust Tony not to reveal his secret hideaway, he could not stop others from stumbling across his camp, and when Blough and Tim did so they immediately told Stuart, who was that week's leader. After that, it was brought to the attention of the whole cast, who had mixed reactions to the news.

Some thought it was quite cool, and others wanted to copy the idea. Kev was pissed off about not knowing about it, apart from anything else: 'I was shocked that someone went off without any of us knowing – it's really sneaky. I thought we were supposed to be a group, and that we should live and

'That's really why I want to go on my own – to see if I can survive.'
D

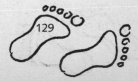

129

Tony

Best:

Getting utterly wrecked on the plane on the way over. (Can that one count, as we weren't strictly ship-wrecked at that point? I'll do one extra, just in case.)

Being voted as leader in the first week and the responsibilities that went with it.

Seeing the most beautiful fish I have ever seen... and then killing them.

All the girls having their boobs out... all the time.

Every night having the opportunity to sit and watch the most fantastic, untainted sunset one could ever hope for.

Jody. (Ahhhh!)

Worst:

Wanting to throttle and maim ordinarily reasonable people.

'Loo-paper' that smears instead of absorbs – Andrex tree my arse... I got more off with a bus ticket once!

All the fish that I never caught... next time... next time.

The 'sand in the bottom of the sleeping bag' mystery. Like the mystery of the pubic hair, no one will ever know how it got there.

Leaving the island – the saddest day of my life so far.

survive as a group. Now a lot of people are saying they want their own shelters and they are going to build huts and tree houses.' Others were irritated when they discovered that D had walked off with two sheets of corrugated iron which they needed for the main hut. Andy and Jody had asked D to help them look for some to waterproof the roof, but he told them he had already looked and there was none on the island, 'and then we find his hut and there's sheets of it.' The boys really felt it was as if D was sticking two fingers up at the group.

Emma-Rosa spoke for a number of the cast when she said: 'Of course he's entitled to his own space, but if he had told us first perhaps we wouldn't have felt the way we did when we first found out. Now other people are saying they want to build their own shelters. I was happy the way the group had gelled and stayed together, so I felt very deflated when I heard about this. I was counting on everything staying the same. I know we all need privacy, and it is a long time to have all these people in your face. If I want isolation I will go for a walk on my own, but I don't want to sleep on my own. Me and Samara do not want to be left on our own without the lads in the camp.'

Stuart confessed that he was actually bothered by D's camp: 'I know some people don't mind, but I do. On coming to this island I knew I would have to forfeit my personal space and I thought everyone else would accept that too. But it's strange when you are forced to realize that even in

'I think the camp is in danger of becoming segregated.'
Emma-Rosa

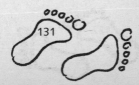

a group as small as this, people have quite different and quite definite opinions. People, of course, need different things, and what this has shown up is that some of us want physical space and others mental space.'

But tension continued to increase within the group. Kev was feeling particularly edgy, desperate to do something for the group, for the community, and finding his exclusion distressing. Even though he liked Jody, he was building up a great deal of resentment over the fact that Jody was the one working on the boat: 'It's always Jody this and Jody that if anything needs doing, why doesn't somebody say, "Let Kev do this, let Kev build the boat."' One evening while attempting to help with the petrol lamps, he knocked one over and nearly burned down the communal camp, which didn't help...

Nerves were already frayed enough by the time the programme's Executive Producer David Frank arrived from London. The cast warily tried to assess whether he was there to observe, or whether there was a more specific purpose behind the visit. They found out soon enough when David called them together and solemnly announced that they were about to receive their last delivery of supplies. From now on they would have to fetch them from the mainland themselves. They were allowed two attempts to reach the mainland and bring back food and supplies – but no more. If they don't make it on either occasion – tough! If the boat sinks – tougher!

Once the bombshell sank in, there was uproar – everyone wanted to go on the ration run, but there was only room for two people each time. They would therefore have to vote for their four crusaders. Kev wasn't the only one to get wound up about the process – Samara too was desperate to be a contender: 'It's stamina, not strength that will count on the journey. I would really like to go, but I won't be 'cos they don't hold a very good opinion of me. I can do this, I know I can – it's so frustrating.'

Over on another part of the island, Kev was less than happy before the votes were taken: 'The minute it was announced, everybody said Jody was a must, 'cos he made the boat. Jody was leader, Jody did the hut, Jody made the boat… [but] I really want to go and if I don't get to go it won't be good for me. Neither do I want to sound sexist but it's going to be a male thing – simply because it's about strength and stamina.'

And then, of course, there's D – as the great Australian male he was sure he was the best man for the job . But once the votes were cast (and they were close, particularly for the second run), the chosen four were Jody and Tim, and then Andy and Kev. D tried to put a brave face on rejection (not too successfully), while the winners were relieved to be chosen. In the end, though, Tim surprised everyone by making the ultimate sacrifice for his friend, handing his place on the first ration run over to D.

The mood on the island shifted with the arrival of Ernie and their last supplies, plus their luxury, a map. Instantly, they deduce that it's for hidden treasure, and before long they had found their buried gold – five bottles of rum! Bickering and arguing erupted as to how much they should drink then and how much to save for later. Tempers were frayed, and emotions running high, so Stuart as leader called a meeting to choose how and what to drink – much to Blough's frustration. He had more than had enough of the number of meetings being held all the time. For rum, however, he was willing to make an exception, and decided to attend and vote. Eventually, they voted for a party, which had some surprising consequences…

BLOUGH'S DIARY

Got the shelter finished yesterday. Pissed off with some people 'cos they're not pulling their weight. Had our first row on camera yesterday with Lucy lesbian about her gay flag – stupid, really. I bet U any money that makes the show. Feeling good today, sitting on the beach writing this. Being here has made me realize it's time for me to grow up and get out on my own two feet.

Me, Andy + Tony killed two chickens today; it was horrible. The killing was bad enough, but the gutting was even worse. Me and Andy took care of it all + no-one helped us; they didn't even give us any extra chicken at dinner.

Andy, Kev + Tony have a massive fallout with the Australian girls over some sexist comments + the girls threaten to leave the island. It all blows over later on + everyone's friends again. I'm feeling really happy and good.

Tony finds out that Lucy's still slagging him off + decides to bring it up in front of the whole group and the cameras. It doesn't go particularly well + no-one likes the tension very much. I get a bit depressed after dinner and go to the beach alone. Samara joins me after about thirty minutes. I see a side of her I didn't know existed. She completely changes my opinion of her. Tony says he is going to leave because of how Lucy is making him feel. Then they meet on the beach and have a row; he decides to sleep on the beach.

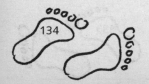

Me, Andy + Kev get interviewed together and it's quite amusing. Then I do the shipwreck rap in front of the cameras, with Tim and Andy on backing vocals. We do it about six times from loads of different angles and everyone seems to love it. Everyone keeps telling me how much weight I'm losing, even though I can't see it. I guess I'll find out when I get home. I'm growing close to Lucy from Blackpool, which is funny because I didn't think we'd get on.

Went to the mainland and spoke to Mum. Things don't sound too good for Nan, but they all want me to stay out here. It was great to have a chance to speak to Mum. I had breakfast afterwards + I had two sausages, two bacon, scrambled egg, tomatoes, two slices of toast, a muffin, a can of coke, a milkshake – needless to say, it was lovely. Everyone back at camp was waiting for me when I got back – they all said they really missed me, which was nice. They were all jealous about the food I had.

Feeling homesick for the first time today. This is the longest I've been away [from home], and it feels like it. I've got to help the girls kill the chickens this afternoon – that should be fun. I slept on the beach for the first time last night and loved it. This evening it all came out again about Lucy M stealing food from the crew camp.

We find five bottles of rum in our treasure hunt and decide to have a bit of a party. It starts well and gets better, I get a little kiss off Lucy T and then Samara + then I got it on with Larissa, even though it's more like she got it on with me. Stuart and Lucy M throw up and I have to help Stuart to the toilet... not pretty.

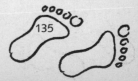

WEEK 6

Monday *Have never been so hungry*

Tuesday *Party!*

Wednesday *Hangover*

Thursday *Lads stealing rum*

Friday *Leader Stuart holds vote for ration runs*

Saturday *D went mad - not chosen*

Sunday *Tan coming along v. well*

A stay on a desert island sounds idyllic to most people. Miles away from every hassle and worry. Lying in the sun, surrounded by clear blue waters and bright blue skies, accessorized by swaying palms, getting to know a group of strangers, would give anybody a chance to either let their true personality shine through or perhaps completely reinvent themselves. What nobody could have anticipated was what this mix of solitude and peer pressure could do to a person's psyche. Most of the shipwreckees, even the strongest, found the most difficult thing to cope with on the island was not the food deprivation, nor the nightly invasions of mosquitoes, nor indeed the horrors of the long-drop, but the proximity of other people. The total invasion of personal space. All of the group found it difficult to understand that even with just seventeen people on an island, that could sometimes be sixteen too many.

In the early days, it resulted in childish spats – even though at the time they seemed serious – about who was nicking biscuits, who wasn't doing their fair share of work and who was playing up in front of the cameras. Occasionally, they turned into full-scale rows, based on sexism and racism, as when the Aussie girls went to pieces listening to the Brit lads extolling their pub philosophy on what women were best for, or when Lucy M attacked public schoolboy Tony for what she termed his out-and-out sexist views. While the former disagreement was quickly patched up and forgotten about, the latter continued to simmer slowly, never quite healing. As time went on, the hurt and bewilderment lessened, but the motivation behind it was never far away from the surface.

But life goes on. And life had to go on on Nuku – there were still fish to be caught, vegetables to be tended and a boat to be mended. Normal social intercourse needed to continue. The bitterness and harsh feelings had to be put away. And anyway,

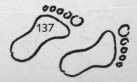

the sun was shining, the sea was inviting and suntans needed to be worked on! Yet throughout their sojourn, every so often something would happen to remind the cast of just how fragile their island existence was. First it was Vic's departure, so soon after the arrival. It really shocked a number of the cast, especially when they realized just how easy it would be for them to go home too. But they became even more fragmented once D's hut was discovered. This was the blueprint of what life could be like on the island – you could be there as part of the programme, or experiment, depending on your point of view, but you could also be apart from the main group.

Vic's departure led people to question their own needs and strengths. Did they all have to stay in one place, or did they choose to? Were they strong enough to survive a group? Did they have what it took to live on their own? Did they have the guts to make a stand or to be unpopular? Just when each member of the group thought they had their task sussed, something else would come along to make them question everything all over again.

Most of them muddled through, many enjoying the solitude and the trials, others remembering that the whole thing was all finite and that there were just a few more weeks to go. But the whole group realized in the end that only by acknowledging their weaknesses would they have the strength to survive and to enjoy their magical adventure. One of the most positive people throughout the whole experience was Stuart. His natural exuberance as a performer helped cheer people up and jolly them along. Coupled with his caring nature and his no-nonsense Mancunian upbringing, it made him a firm favourite with his co-shipwreckees. So it was hardly surprising that he had been voted in as leader, something which he confessed he was both thrilled and flattered about. 'I can't say it's because I'm popular, it's not that,' he reasoned, 'it's just that I attract warmth and people want to be around me. Everybody here is longing for stability: just as the weather lurches from sun to rain, people here are lurching from high drama to boredom. But I'm lucky – I am seen as a mediator. I came here to get to know myself, but I am also getting to know a lot about other people.'

'The guys can talk to me and the girls can talk to me.'
Stuart

But despite his capacity for understanding and his positive approach to everything, Stuart also had his private demons, which he did not admit to until the middle of his leadership. It was all very well keeping everybody buoyant and active, but what happened when the lights went down and the audience went home?

Stuart went to the hut-cam in the middle of the night and revealed how he was really feeling. 'Everyone's asleep and I have had to come to talk about my loneliness,' he began, tentatively. 'I don't want to talk to the others about it in case they think I am looking for sympathy. I don't know why I feel like this – I have been lonely before, I'm an only child – but this time I am emotionally rather than just physically lonely. Perhaps that is something for me to learn. And because I am the only gay guy here I suppose that makes everything else very intense and lonely. I'm not lonely during the day because there is so much to do and I am making lots of friends. But at night – when I'm on my own – that's different. I miss emotional warmth and friendship.' But you can't keep a good man down, for in the very

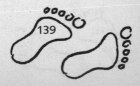

next breath Stuart admitted, 'There's a lot of love here and it makes me happy. I may be emotionally lonely, but the whole experience will make me a lot stronger.'

The other person who was going through a personal crisis at this point was Larissa. From the beginning she had had a succession of illnesses – everything from colds and hangovers to aches and sunburn. The latter earned her very little sympathy, particularly from urbanites such as Stuart: 'We're city people,' he argued, '[the Aussies are] used to the bush and the ocean and the great outdoors. Larissa can't have got sunburn – she's Australian.' There were days when she had to stay in bed because she felt so unwell, even worrying at one point that malnutrition might set in. Her emotional health fared no better, and she was the first to be affected by the boys' sexist remarks. Larissa struck up a close friendship with Jody, spending much of her time alone with him. Nevertheless, she was always acutely conscious that she had left a boyfriend back home – a boyfriend with whom she had a number of unresolved issues, but still someone she did not want to offend or humiliate by being seen making out with another guy on television. Larissa was a complex woman, and by her sixth week on the island she was also a confused one.

Her frustration with the place and the people really began to

'I have never felt as lonely as I do right now.'

Stuart

show itself after D's hut was discovered. Her fellow Australian was confronted with the group's views about it at a public meeting during one of the mealtimes. Larissa felt it was neither right nor proper to wade in on D like this. She felt it would have been better if the leader had had a quiet chat with D first to ascertain why he had felt the need to take such a step. 'Once again everything is ruled by meetings,' she complained. 'This group love humiliation, it's their number one tool. I feel like people are part of a jury here and you have to stand up and defend yourself – it annoys the shit out of me.

'The rest of the time I feel as if I'm in a strict boarding school being told how to go to the toilet,' she continued. 'It's all about the group and so little about the individual. Yesterday, for instance, we were given a lecture about how to go the toilet, how to put things back where we find them, how to wash our own cup and plate. I find the whole thing offensive. I'm an independent person who has lived by myself since I was seventeen. I know how to wash my plate and how to go to the toilet. I am a twenty-three year-old feeling like I am doing time here, as if my life is on hold, while I sit on this island doing nothing apart from a TV show, which wasn't the point for me.

'I have a job, a flat; everything I love is at home and here I feel like I am waiting, counting the days till I can start my life again,' she moaned. 'My idea of coming here was to see how I could survive in adversity and test the theory of a group of people living together. But all of this has dissolved and I don't like the way it's going. For some people the point of coming here is to be on TV; for others, it's getting a suntan. I don't feel free here and it's the group that's causing that – not just the TV cameras watching us.'

Larissa's boredom and frustration increased and came to a

> '**I am fed up with being spoken to like a fifteen-year-old.**'
> *Larissa*

head the night the group found hidden treasure. Each week a number of luxury items were set before them so that they could vote for one to come with Ernie on their ration run. Fed up with being sensible and asking for fishing nets, oars and nails, one week they opted for a map. No one knew the significance of the map – what it showed or what it offered. But when it arrived it soon became pretty obvious that its great gift was the offer of treasure. The cast pored over it, following dud clues and missing the more obvious ones. In the end, sixteen great minds won through and the cast rushed to the place where the treasure was hidden, digging it up as fast as they possibly could. And what did the sand spill forth? Five bottles of rum. What could any self-respecting group of shipwreckees do, but immediately start to party…?

It was a party like no other on the island. The rum was drunk quickly – most of it neat, and some of it mixed with coconut milk into cocktails. Beth was one of the few who stayed almost sober: 'I didn't drink a lot because on previous occasions I drank quite a lot and chucked loads up. This time I just held the bucket for those being sick or helped clear it up – loads were being sick in the tent. I saw a lot of things happen. Larissa just went mad, absolutely crazy,' she recalled. 'She was going in and out of the water and then she was steaming around shouting and screaming at everybody.'

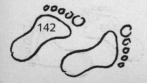

Larissa

Best:

Meeting new people and forming friendships in adversity (especially Jody, Lisa, Tony, Lucy M).

All the time I had to think about my life, my dreams and what really counts.

Learning survival on a desert island.

Learning that I can survive without food, sex and cigarettes and coming home skinny and brown. Shipwrecked was the ultimate health retreat!

The beauty of our island.

Worst:

Being hungry all the time (I lost over five kilos).

Never being clean or comfortable. No bed, no showers, no toilet, no couch.

Getting sick (I got a kidney infection caused by dehydration, and felt like I was dying for two weeks).

The debates – I hated it when the whole group got together and picked on one person, or argued just to hear the sound of their own voices.

The cameras – one of the most annoying things was when you were in the middle of a conversation with someone, and suddenly the cameras were there, and then you were totally aware that you didn't want the world to know about your personal business. So you either changed the conversation, or completely forgot what you were talking about in the first place. It's pretty hard to just 'be yourself' when you don't really want complete strangers to know everything about you.

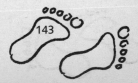

143

One of those people Larissa offended was Beth herself, by shouting out that she was 'the spawn of the devil'. But she didn't stop there! She then shrieked her dislike for the Brits and how they were the ones who were making her sick. Speaking of which, in the meantime half the cast joined in the pukeathon. Stuart had to be put to bed by Tim and Beth, while Lucy M was also rather unwell. In-between all of this, Larissa managed to insult Jody and Lisa quite badly. D and Lisa were trying to look after her but in the end D gave up and went back to his hut in disgust. Tim took on the role of comforting Lisa. He had become cross with Larissa's attack on the Brits and also defended Lisa when Larissa went banging on about Greeks in another of her drunken rants.

'I think she offended a lot of people.' *Beth*

In spite of being upset by her attack, Lisa was very sympathetic to Larissa the following morning. 'Most people got drunk and Larissa got very drunk and went a bit crazy. I think she needed to, she was really stressed out that day and it gave her a chance to let off some steam,' she reasoned. 'Jody and I spent the night looking out for her. It was a pretty full-on night and it went on for hours [as we were] following her up and down the beach.

'She's been ill a lot out here. Every other day there's something wrong, and I think that's got a lot to do with the fact that because she doesn't feel emotionally strong her immune system

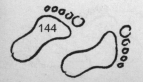

isn't coping. The food's bad, it takes a lot of strength to stay on top of things, but she's unwell. The hangover was self-inflicted but I don't think she's pretending to be sick, I think she believes she's not well.'

Jody was just as sympathetic. 'The only people that I can remember her being offensive to were probably only Lisa and myself. I mean, a lot of it was drunken nonsense, but she said a couple of things that were quite cutting and directed at me. But I'm sure she didn't mean them. A lot of people were genuinely shocked at such a character shift – they said she was possessed. I've been around a lot of drunks but I've never seen anybody react quite that strongly to alcohol. It was incredible and quite upsetting,' he admitted. 'I know a few things have been bothering her and she probably meant to get drunk but got drunk for the wrong reasons. But she expects too much, she expects everything to come to her, when in real life you've got to make these things work for you.'

Jody was still one of the first people to see Larissa the following morning, when she told him she hadn't meant a thing she'd said the previous night. However, some of the others weren't so sure. Emma-Rosa had little sympathy for Larissa when the following morning she complained of a cold as well as a hangover: 'She made herself really sick and now she's back to square one, she's sick again – Miss Queen!' Samara's view was that Larissa was used to a lot of attention but wasn't getting enough from the group, who were all quite strong and quite attention seeking themselves. 'She's not getting the sympathy that she used to get,' she argued, 'and I'm not saying that she hasn't been sick, but neither am I saying that some of it isn't played up.'

But both Jody and Lisa had an insight into what was going on in Larissa's mind. Jody's hope was 'that she can step back and realize what an amazing experience this is and how lucky

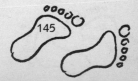

we are to be here and that she has got to take everything she can away from here. But then if she's not enjoying herself there is no reason to stay.' For her part, Lisa reckoned that Larissa no longer wanted to be on the island at all: 'I suspected she was unhappy after the first couple of weeks and then she told me she was unhappy five days ago and that did shock me. D and I obviously don't want her to go, and we still believe that it's the three of us and we can stick it out. She's not like Vic, who was young and feeling isolated. She's the kind of person who could cope, who could get through the misery because she will come out better for it. Vic had more to gain by going home early, but I don't think Larissa will.'

The subject of discussion had taken her hangover to another part of the island to reflect and collect her faculties, but there was an air of inevitability about the outcome of her musings. The following morning, Larissa confessed that she felt like an animal in a zoo, no longer able to cope with cameras, feeling trapped and an unwilling participant in a social experiment. 'I don't have the kind of personality to be in front of the camera the whole time,' she confessed. 'I think acting and doing this is totally different. I've done acting, so I thought I'd feel happy about doing this, but I don't. I think Jody, D and Lisa know pretty much how I feel. I've had a chat with Lisa and I know she doesn't want me to leave. She thinks it would be good for me to stay. I, however, know myself better, and would regret staying for five weeks when I know my family and friends would be saying "Why didn't you come home?" I know we are only three Aussies and that the others don't want me to go, and I wouldn't if I thought they wouldn't survive without me. But they will and personally I've already got what I want out of it.

'Five days from now I'd like to be sitting in my sitting room on a couch with my family and friends.' But would she? Would Larissa

really be able to say goodbye to the cast, the cameras and the island? The production crew refused to help her, but she managed to persuade D and Jody to take her over to Fukave on the boat, where she can try and hitch a ride with a local fisherman. Larissa shared her decision and plans, but decided a little later not to go until after D's birthday. Was her little version of the waiting game another pitch for attention? The lads thought so. When it came to the crunch, was Larissa herself serious enough, and brave enough, to go through with it and wait for a lift on another island, all on her own?

'I'm not happy, and I haven't been for weeks.' Larissa

In the meantime, the lads were getting bored and mischievous. They decided to steal and drink the half bottle of rum left from the treasure hunt. For the best part of a day they thought they'd got away with, blaming their half-cut state on smoking rolled up banana leaves! However, the next day, while relaxing on the Beautiful Man Beach the lads were confronted by Tim, angry, hurt and disappointed with them for stealing from the group – it's every bit as bad as stealing from your own family, he claimed, accusing them of betraying the trust the group need to have in each other. Tim then told Andy that he felt so strongly about the deceit that if he had to vote again for the ration run duo he would no longer vote for him.

Both Andy and Kev were stunned at his reaction – even more so when Stuart, as leader, called a meeting to discuss whether a breakdown in trust had really taken place and how it affected

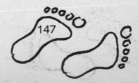

the trip to the mainland that the two lads were voted in for. The ensuing meeting called for a re-vote, much to the lads' horror. Andy resigned himself to expect the worst, while Kevin lost his temper and threatened all kinds of emotional blackmail before storming out, almost in tears. He was followed by Tim, who tried to calm him down, pointing out that he was doing his cause no good by reacting in such a childish way, and should go back and apologize to Stuart for his behaviour. Eventually, Tim's words had an effect. Jo, meanwhile, turned on Andy and Kev in front of the group, excoriating their behaviour and making it clear that she would not be voting for either of them this time around.

In an extraordinarily tense moment, a secret ballot was taken and everyone held their breath while Stuart counted the votes. There was a palpable sense of relief when, after a close count, Kev and Andy were actually reinstated. Now, things could get back to normal. Or could they?

It was all very well having decided on the two ration runs, but what about the boat? Fragile and home-made, could it possibly survive the long journey through the reef and into choppy waters? There was only one way to tell and it was time for the *Victoria* to be launched into the great South Pacific ocean.

GOING OFF-ISLAND

While the reality that the island of Nuku presented was beyond every cast member's wildest dreams, they were all still subject to that primeval longing for home as they gazed across the beautiful blue sea toward the nearest land mass. The grass is always greener! They also clung to the idea of escape – escape both from the cameras and from each other's prying eyes. Each member of the group was allowed one night alone, away from the sometimes suffocating proximity of the others. According to their contract they could escape, albeit briefly, either alone or with one other person, to Fukave.

Swimming or rowing to Fukave, with a crew member along for safety reasons but no cameras in tow, the castaway could have one night of freedom. No questions asked, no reports expected. So tempting – and yet most of them flunked it...

The idea of Fukave as Love Island, a romantic retreat, was doomed from the start. Sure, the castaways swam across and explored during the day, but they showed little interest in spending the night there, particularly in pairs! It might have been different if most of the group hadn't left partners behind at home – and if they hadn't seen the islanders in the first series of *Shipwrecked* publicly jeopardize their relationships. This time, they were all too aware that what might be an entirely innocent scene in context could play out very differently at home, thousands of miles away in cold, damp Britain. Apart from some mild flirtation and a few playful snogs, everyone was very well-behaved.

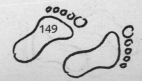

In several cases, the cast were already worried enough about whether their relationships could stand the strain of such a long separation, and gossip was rife. The first duo to stir up speculation were Jody and Larissa, who bonded almost instantly on the island of Tonga and were near inseparable for the first few weeks on Nuku. And, as Larissa confessed to the hut-cam, 'It's a very romantic place, which makes it very easy to forget what's at home.' But, like a whopping thirteen of her team-mates, Larissa had a partner back at home and a relationship she wasn't willing to give up on quite that easily. 'I have a boyfriend, Aaron, and we've been together for eight months,' she revealed. 'However, our relationship is a bit rocky, and we have almost split up, and this time on Nuku gives us a bit of a break, because we have a lot of issues to resolve.'

Larissa was so concerned about being straight with Aaron that she was determined not to rock the boat, and when her attachment with Jody began to look as though it might get a little heavier, she deliberately backed off. 'Jody and I are pretty close, but because of Aaron I don't want to get any closer,' she affirmed. 'Out of respect for Aaron I don't want to start something with somebody on the other side of the world.' Suddenly, the chances of much romantic trysting on Fukave or anywhere else seemed worlds away...

The ration runs also took two teams off the island, for two and three nights respectively. The first pair were very responsible, staying at the cheapest backpackers' hostel they could find – leaking roof and all. The second team were even cannier, managing to find Ernie and stay with him!

A different kind of escape also became available, when a few emergencies arose during the shoot and various people were taken off the island and allowed a few precious hours on the mainland. An unlucky accident caused D's away-day when he

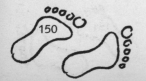

trod on a rusty nail and the crew thought it best to have a medic look at it immediately rather than wait for the weekly doctor's rounds, in case of infection. During the very last week, Lucy M managed to knock herself out and had to be checked for concussion – 'It was so stupid. I was helping to put a hut together, stood up and hit my head on a tree. It was a heavy blow, but I did it again a second time, and that time I knocked myself out.'

Blough had to be whisked off island a couple of times on missions of mercy. Just before he left England, he learned that his gran had been diagnosed with cancer, so he was very worried about her right from the start. Coming from a single-parent family, Blough feels a great sense of responsibility toward his gran, mum and sister, and even arranged for his mates to help them with shopping and jobs around the house while he was away. A couple of weeks after they arrived on Nuku, the *Shipwrecked* production office received a call from Blough's mum, explaining that his gran's condition had deteriorated and that she would like to speak to her son and tell him about it. The crew immediately took him off the island to make the call from a telephone on the mainland. He offered to return home, but his mum wouldn't hear of it, and insisted that his gran wanted him to see the ten weeks through.

Three weeks later, Blough's mother called again to say his gran was, unfortunately, getting worse, and that she had only been given a matter of months to live. Blough was taken to a phone for the second time to talk to his family, but again they reassured him that they wanted him to stay put.

For Blough, apart from speaking to his loved ones, the only good thing about his trips off-island was that each time he got to eat something other than cabbage and rice, since he was missing lunch on the island. In one over-tense moment, Lucy T

claimed it was unfair that Blough was having access to proper food when she wasn't, thereby causing a huge row between them. Very quickly, however, Lucy cooled off and accepted that Blough's reason for leaving the island was unique and couldn't have been foreseen by anyone.

And Fukave? The only other team members to leave the island during their stay were the group of boys who headed off together towards the end of their stay to spend a night on the island away from the girls, doing whatever it is boys do. Romantic, it wasn't!

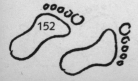

WEEK 7

Monday *Food getting scarce*

Tuesday *Larissa wants to leave*

Wednesday *Working on the boat*

Thursday *Cabbage and rice, rice and cabbage and a few bits of bony fish*

Friday *Andy ill*

Saturday *Swimming. Nice.*

Sunday *Rice. Oh dear.*

Whoever would have thought that after seven weeks on Nuku the main topic of conversation, concern and unrest would still be food? As well as the lack of it, the limited choice and the boredom generated by constant rice and cabbage, a new wave of panic hit our castaways over the ration runs. Would they be able to make it to the mainland – would their oh-so-fragile-looking boat be able to withstand the waves? And if the first run did make it to the mainland, would they ever get back?

The very air surrounding the island seemed filled with uncertainties – and not just about future food supplies. In fact, by now the cast had started questioning themselves, their motives and their relationships... and each other. Lucy T, normally the most cheery member of the group, was beginning to get fed up with the constant moaning and the constant emphasis on the lack of sex and the lack of sustenance. 'Everyone's driving me crazy talking about sex and food,' she griped. 'We're all torturing ourselves really badly. Larissa is annoying a lot of people. I know we all got drunk on Wednesday night, but she was hurling abuse at absolutely everyone.'

'Even the weather's been bad – Ernie said it was something to do with the moon.'
Lucy T

And even though she is a happy-go-lucky character by nature, Lucy T admitted that she had her moments of feeling low and frustrated, especially when 'I can't get away from people who get so mad over the smallest things. I'm not an argumentative person, but being in an atmosphere when people argue over two crackers and have to have meetings about who takes two steps to the left of the island before someone else... it's all so annoying. People are beginning to show their tempers and that stresses others out and then I feel like a caged animal under surveillance the whole time.'

Lucy also confessed to the hut-cam that she was worried about the ration run: 'I think it's going to be a lot harder than people think – it's four miles across really strong currents. Ernie says it will take about six hours, but [the lads] are saying it will only be three – get real!'

Even Jo, one of the most equable cast members, was getting fed up with the petty arguments and constant discussions. 'I'm tired of leaders and being told what to do,' she revealed, 'and I find myself getting uptight and snappy... I'm even starting to get fed up with good friends I've made.' That's why Jo felt that it was imperative for her to get her shelter finished, so that she could move in and try and be self-sufficient for the last part of the stay. By now, Larissa was seriously annoying Jo. 'She's been sick since she got here. Not sure she really is sick or just attention getting,' Jo mused. 'She really has cried wolf a lot. I think it's an excuse for her to mope around and get sad. I know she wishes for a major storm to hit us so that it's not safe for us to stay here and we will have to be shipped out. She makes me feel angry for wasting this opportunity and I don't want to be around people who make me feel like that.'

But by now, Larissa had finally decided to go and persuaded both Jody and D to take her to the next island in the boat with all her stuff, from where she hoped to hitch a ride with some locals. Before she went she made one last attempt to justify her actions to the hut-cam. 'I have got a lot out of coming here,' she insisted. 'One of the main things I have found out is that I

155

can live on rice, mackerel and cabbage... and not go mad. Never thought I could live without eating the amounts I usually do. I've also learnt that most people can learn to live without bed, only being able to wash in the ocean, no hot water and being attacked by mosquitoes twenty-four hours a day. I now know that happiness doesn't equate to physical things.

'Talking about food just makes me bloody hungry.' Jody

'Everything here seems a lot bigger, small things get magnified,' Larissa commented. 'I know me leaving is going to seem [like a big deal] at the time, but I love my life and freedom too much to want to stay here and play the TV game. People really haven't had a chance to get to know me and vice versa – and others won't even know each other [by the time] they leave. A lot of people here are on their best behaviour because of the camera and they know we're going to be judged by thousands of people... but for others, this is how we really are. I'm a very private person and I want to keep it like that, which is why I have trouble being around a camera...'

Larissa's greatest fan was Jody, but even he became exasperated with some of her views. 'This island gives back to people who have given to it and for Larissa to sit back and say she doesn't like the conversation means she is expecting too much from people and is expecting everything on a plate,' he insisted. 'I know it drives me mad too, but what do you expect when you get fifteen people from such different backgrounds? The only

156

conversations they are going to have as a group are basica[lly] [going to be about] sex, TV and food. I know conversation. about sex should be saved for one person in particular, and that's it. If Larissa thinks that conversation is going to come to her 'cos she's not happy, then she is mistaken.'

And so the frustration and boredom went round and round. One thing that stirred them out of the straitjacket was the day

---

Beth

Best:

Total peace from anything mechanical (ie cars, planes and buses).

Time to both think about things and relax completely.

Getting to know sixteen people who all individually are fantastic people – even though sometimes you can have too much of something that is too good. And staying friends with them.

Getting pissed on the island was really good, because you always had at least five people looking after you (including sick boy – Timmy Ra: he always looked after the ones who were being sick) and I couldn't think of a more perfect place to have a hangover.

The weather/experience/ island was just perfect. I wouldn't have changed anything for the world. It is something that I had the greatest pleasure to be involved in, and I would do it again at the drop of a hat – but next time, don't make us go home.

Worst:

The cameras when you are trying to have either a private or sad moment.

No contact with my family (I especially missed my brother and sister).

NO SWEETS (I really craved those pink-and-white milkshake bottles from Woolworths).

It all went too quickly!

Not being able to see certain people every day now that I am back. (Stuart and Tim).

that Larissa really did leave. In spite of their different views about her and the impact she had made on the island, it was still a wrench for the last fifteen to see her go. There were some careful goodbyes, but a few tearful ones too before Larissa set off with D and Jody for the next island. There was an extra dimension to this venture – it was also the canoe's first proper outing. And it didn't take long for the two oarsmen to realize that the boat was in trouble; almost within a stone's throw of Nuku they were forced to begin baling out. Worrying enough for the relatively short twenty-minute journey to the neighbouring island, but the cast were already thinking of Ernie's estimation that it would take six hours to reach the mainland. From the beaches the remaining castaways could almost see the shock on Larissa's face and the serious expression on D's. The farther they went out, the higher the waves seemed; their little bit of flotsam was being buffeted about like a paper sail. At one stage, to the horror of those watching, the boat appeared to be about to go under completely, along with its three passengers.

Eventually, exhausted and drenched, they arrived at the is[...]
Within minutes they had found a fisherman's boat that was tak[...]
off to the mainland and begged a lift for Larissa. After that, t[...]
boys had no alternative but to head back, in a much less confiden[...]
style, to Nuku. But the mood had changed in paradise: all of a
sudden, reality had set in. The cast had seen how difficult it was
just to get to the nearest island on their flimsy boat. They had
watched for weeks as Jody had done everything within his power
and remit to ensure that the vessel was seaworthy and now, at
last, they had seen just how fragile it was. Serious doubts were
suddenly raised about the viability of a ration run. Lisa and Emma
started budgeting rations for the remaining weeks so that if the
run didn't happen or didn't work there was still some food left.
Beth hightailed it to the garden to see what was left and what
they could hope for. Of course, they all knew that coconuts and
papayas were there for the asking. But you needed to shin up a
tree of thirty or so feet to reach the coconuts, and you had to be
sure the papayas were ripe before eating them. And there were
plenty of fish down in the ocean, but most of the cast still had not
realized just how difficult it is to persuade fish to leave the deep
to line hungry stomachs. And that realization dawned roughly
around the same time that the regular fisherman, Tony and Jody,
were getting just a bit bored with the onus always being on them
to provide food…

To underline their point of view, the two lads made a raft to
which they could attach nightlines out on the reef. That way
anyone could swim out and check for fish, which meant that it
wouldn't always be down to the same handful of people to
provide a new catch. Tony explained: 'Now that we know we
will have to fish a lot more, as our rations are depleting and none
of us know whether D and Jody will make it, so the food
situation is quite dangerous, which is why fishing is so important.

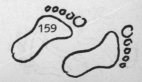

or the first three weeks, me and Jody spent three to four urs a day on the reef and [were] quite a success, with between x and eight fish a day. It gets very cold and very boring out .here and people weren't really appreciative of our efforts. It's also very hard work because of the currents – we'd bring back fish and nobody would either acknowledge [our work] or say thanks. Now we have these nightlines, I'll show them where they are and where the bait is... I'm happy to teach them so now they can go out and get fish themselves.' With this extra aid in place and with the existing supplies divided up for each week, the cast decided to abandon all thoughts of a ration run and see if they could still survive.

A great idea, but with fifteen jittery and edgy shipwreckees worrying about food and panicking about survival, how long could they stick it out? Nerves that were getting jangled before were now exposed, raw and aching. Lucy T and Samara were now well and truly fed up with the lads taking the mickey out of them. 'People think of us as easy targets,' Lucy T complained. 'We know it's only joking, but now it's getting to us. They call us slags and other sexual things – it's not very nice. I thought they were my friends, but friends would stop this behaviour when they see it's hurting.'

'I'm really fond of Andy and Blough, but they are a nightmare together.'

LUCY T

Samara felt exactly the same: 'At first it was easy for them to take the mickey, 'cos Lucy and I were laughing along with them,'

she observed, 'but now they're getting personal, nasty and r
I've already pulled Andy aside and told him I don't like the w
he talks to me.'

In-between all of this, Jo was getting on with building her own hut and at one stage, when Andy became ill (from either too much sun, bad food or mosquitoes) Kev and Blough took him down to Jo's place to help him recover. The two lads were concerned and conscientious about Andy's welfare, bringing him food and water when he needed it, but it was the peace and calm of Jo's hut (called Kenneth, after her dad) that really helped speed the healing process. However, Andy's recuperation was very nearly brought to an abrupt end when Jo discovered that the two lads had been peeing outside her hut. This laddishness is exactly what she had been trying to get away from, a carelessness about other people's needs, feelings and space. Jo ripped into the two guys, leaving them shamefaced and guilty.

The following morning they decided to make amends and whipped into action, clearing the area around Kenneth, bringing pebbles and shells from the beach to line pathways and finding plants and flowers inland to make an impromptu garden. The result was enchanting, but the atmosphere on the island still remained tinged with sourness. Lisa put her finger on it with a comment she made when she resigned from cooking: 'The whole mood is changing; even the cooking has become irritating because the community changes. Nobody is considerate or says thank you. Jody and Tony feel it: they are fed up with getting no credit for all the fishing they've done. They too have decided to become more selfish. It is the natural progression for a community to fall apart and I suppose it's quite odd that we stayed together for as long as we did. And in many ways the lack of community goals makes Nuku more fun for the individual.'

ut then even individuals have to eat, and eventually, as the ather appeared to be getting better and brighter, it was ecided that a ration run might be the way to restore dignity and civility to the island and its inhabitants. D and Jody got themselves ready to go. The mere thought of the run gave everybody a psychological lift, and they started preparing their fantasy shopping lift for the two guys. Andy wanted 'pinky, peppery sauce'; Beth demanded a Tongan man who could swim or be towed behind them, so they would be safe; Lucy M wanted 'ketchup with lesbians dipped in it'; and Kev demanded red wine and baked beans. And *everybody* wanted chocolate. In the end, Jody suggested three lists – one for essentials and the second for luxuries, leaving the more esoteric requests on list three. For a moment morale was high, as the two lads prepared for a good night's sleep before leaving the island. But that boat had looked awfully fragile on its last outing; would they even make it to the mainland?

WEEK 8

Monday *Missing home*

Tuesday *Ration run preparations*

Wednesday *Boat looking dodgy*

Thursday *Boat launched!*

Friday *Everybody wants their own hut*

Saturday *Where are they?*

Sunday *Food!*

preparations were being made for D and Jody to go on first ration run. The weather was unpredictable and everyone was worried for them. The boys decided that rather than head straight for the small gap in the reef, which would have been the quickest way to the mainland but also the place where the waves were biggest and the current strongest, they would do a circuitous tour of the neighbouring islands, sneaking around the currents and headwinds. So that everyone could keep an eye on their progress and safety, they decided that on the first evening they would light a torch and wave towards Nuku.

However, before they could set off, more island business had to be conducted and a new leader had to be voted in. Blough, who was the castaway most fed up with all the rules, restrictions and meetings, decided to run for leader on policies that promised none of the above. His electioneering slogan, 'Vote for the Blough – he's bigger than this whole damn thing', worked, and among much jubilation he was voted in. He proved a popular leader, laid-back and fun. Meetings were cancelled, jobs left undone and idleness and anarchy prevailed. But Blough was insistent about one thing – it was time the girls dug the long-drop. Throughout their stay it had fallen to the boys week after week to do the most disgusting job on the island, and week after week they grumbled but did it. The smell, the flies… in fact, the mere thought of it was nearly as bad as doing it. However, that week Blough's rule as leader was that there would be no more long-drop digs for the boys – and if the girls didn't fulfil their task, he told them that it simply would not be done at all. For days the girls thought Blough might relent and tell them he was joking. But he wasn't, and resolved again not to ask any guy to do it. In the end, the smell was getting so bad that the girls were forced into doing the task themselves – and, to a woman, they

Samara

Best:

Walking around the island with Beth, especially at low tide. We had in-depth relationship conversations and hunted out the red-eye crabs.

Collecting shells and making bracelets and necklaces for friends and family at home.

Living in a house with Lucy T.

Making a chair with Beth. The chair had a back to it so we had something to lean against that was comfortable. We kept it a secret until it was built.

Inventing the game 'Beach Flob' with Tim, Jody and Vic.

Worst:

The mosquitoes.

Digging and using the long-drop.

That I didn't get a chance to row to the mainland for supplies.

That Vic, Larissa and Jo left.

Raining at night when you had to use the long-drop, and there were big drips landing on your sleeping bag and face.

The flies landing on you and waking you up in the mornings doing discos on your forehead.

agreed that it was the vilest thing that existed in the whole world, let alone in paradise. But it was a victory for equality as far as the lads were concerned.

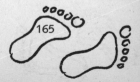

However, a much more dangerous task was about to be attempted, as Jody and D, armed with the shopping list, $300 and a flimsy canoe, headed off on the first great adventure since they arrived on Nuku – the ration run. The whole cast turned out to wave them off, shouting last-minute words of encouragement, instructions and final items for the shopping list. And they remained on the beach for a long time watching the two bob off into the distance, hoping and praying that everything would work out well for them.

The ration runners themselves were cheered and excited by the adventure, D telling Jody, 'I wasn't able to sleep last night, I was so bound up with the thoughts of leaving – and even more so by the idea of a real bed, a big meal and some cold beers.' Jody, on the other hand, found the experience of leaving Nuku very strange. 'I cannot believe that we are heading towards a horizon I've been staring at for the last few weeks,' he reflected.

Things got a little risky when they discovered that they needed to bail out water seeping into the boat – and that was after just thirty minutes at sea. But for once the weather was kind to them and the sea became calmer, so they decided to change their plans and head straight for the mainland, hoping that the calm sea and their home-made sail would both hold until then. Within five hours they hit their destination. Overjoyed, they celebrated with chicken burgers, chips, ice cream and cold beers – and the memory of the fantastic first taste of things they hadn't had for over two months will probably always stay with them.

Meanwhile, back on the island, the rest of the group had the rather more familiar taste of rice and cabbage to relish. As it grew darker, they wandered down to the beach to see if they could see any light coming from the neighbouring islands. Worried that they could see nothing, they brought out a couple of lamps and waved them in roughly the direction of the island.

Then they waited, breathlessly. Eventually another light flash
back at them through the darkness – the remaining castaway
were overjoyed and went back to camp happier and more
relaxed. So desperate were they for a sign that they didn't notice
the light had been green; in fact, it had been sent by some
passing sailors!

D and Jody, meanwhile, had sussed out somewhere to stay –
a somewhat seedy but cheap backpacker's hotel (they were more
than cautious about spending the group's money) and embarked
on their second proper meal. This time it was T-bone steak and
garlic bread, washed down with a number of beers. The number
of beers increased when they met a group of Aussies, who were
fascinated with their story and escapades and insisted on buying
them booze all night long.

Hungover the following morning, the two lads headed off
for the supermarket, determined to accomplish their mission
with all speed and bring proper food back for everyone. But their
wish was thwarted when a violent storm came out of nowhere,
putting paid to any plans they had to return to Nuku that day.
Nothing for it, then, but to retire to the nearest bar and drown
their sorrows. The rest of the cast back on the island were more
than a little worried when they woke up to the storm – their
thoughts were with their two friends, whom they now believed
were stranded on an uninhabited island with no food and no
shelter. They spent the day looking miserable and feeling help-
less, a situation not helped by the fact that there were only fruit
and crackers to eat; fishing was out of the question as the sea
was too turbulent, and the vegetables had almost gone.

Perhaps it was just as well, as the night before Emma-Rosa had
resigned from cooking after a row between herself and Samara.
She had – accidentally or deliberately – put spice in Samara's food,
which the latter couldn't eat. Hunger, boredom and resentment

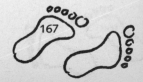

167

...ong the girls had been brewing for some time and this proved ...e point at which it exploded, with both Samara and Lucy T ...elling Emma exactly what they thought of her. According to Lucy M, Emma was genuinely surprised and hurt by what the girls said about her bossiness and general attitude – so much so that she almost cried. It took Stuart to point out that they hadn't really addressed the main reason that people were getting annoyed with her – her camera-grabbing antics.

Lucy M pointed out that the first thing Emma said, rather than 'sorry', was 'I'm going to look such a cow on TV!'

'I'm glad the rest of the group stayed out of it.'
Lucy T

Lucy T had her own, very definite views on Emma-Rosa. 'I never meant to hurt Emma but she has hurt me on many an occasion,' she fumed. 'I don't know how it went but I'm sure it's not going to make much of a difference, she still tried to turn everything round on to Samara and me. She said Samara had done horrible things to her, but she wouldn't say what. Samara surprised me, she was really strong and brave and if it hadn't been for her, I wouldn't have said anything. Jo supported us, and I'm really surprised that Lucy M did, 'cos she's a right gobby cow.'

Beth, on the other hand, managed to maintain her sense of humour about the whole situation. 'Emma-Rosa makes me laugh,' she commented, 'she's so camera-hugging she's ridiculous. She's unbelievable and she doesn't know how to treat people properly.'

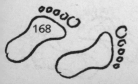

Emma-Rosa

Best:

Meeting the legendary Ernie. He was like a grandfather to me.

Catching an octopus with Tony and Jody on my first time out fishing! I couldn't believe I was holding it and running up the beach with it, making (Tony, Jody and I) cut it up (a weird experience) and frying it with some of my spices (one of my luxury items), oregano and garlic. It was chewy but nice, for a change!

The mini fashion show that Tim and I modelled for. Tim designed and made his own trousers and Jo designed and made my sexy island outfit. It was all made out of this mad red printed material that was provided in our rations. Stuart was our choreographer. It was a laugh and everyone enjoyed the bit of entertainment.

Winding up Kevin by hiding his sleeping bag and getting away with it for three whole weeks before being caught! He got me back by locking me into the hut-cam. It was all just out of boredom and the need to have a bit of fun.

Swimming every morning after my workout in the beautiful turquoise Pacific Ocean. Sometimes it was so clear it was like being in a swimming pool.

Worst:

Saying goodbye to Ernie at Tonga airport. I cried my eyes out. Blough consoled me with one of his big bear hugs.

Being attacked by giant flies and mosquitoes on every visit to our long-drop! You were in trouble if you didn't have repellent on your skin. I was nearly sick the time Stuart, Lucy M and I emptied the thing to make a new long-drop. Yuk!

Samara and I not being such close friends after a stupid girlie fall out. I missed her company and our sister-like fun.

The wild hangovers I would get from the Tongan rum we drank at birthdays. It felt like it burnt holes in your tummy and it also meant visiting the long-drop more often!

Saying goodbye to everyone at Heathrow and knowing I had to go on to Northern Ireland. It was hard because I knew it wasn't as easy for me to see them, because of the distance, and I knew I'd miss everyone like crazy.

Emma, on the other hand, was trying to keep a positive outlook, even though she admitted to feeling really isolated from the other girls on the island. She decided to go off on her own, and headed across the island to D's camp; he had told her she could use it while he was gone. She was relieved on her return when everyone asked her where she had been – at least they had noticed that she'd gone missing and had been worried about her whereabouts.

If nothing else, the Emma-Rosa incident stopped serious boredom from setting in – and for that, most of the cast were

truly grateful. And at last the weather improved, and with the return of the sun they stopped squabbling and got back onto the beach for some more rays or a swim out to the reef. At one point during the day a small dot was seen on the horizon – but they couldn't believe it was D and Jody, whom they still thought were making a roundabout and troubled route to the mainland.

However, they kept an eye on the dot and after an hour or so were convinced it was a local fisherman. But the boat kept on course and was clearly heading their way through the gap on the reef. And, amazingly, it turned out to be the little canoe *Victoria*, and they all zoomed down onto the beach, some of them taking to the water to swim out and welcome the conquering heroes back.

Their joy knew no end as they began to unpack the food – chocolate, pasta, chocolate, wine, chocolate, spicy sauce, chocolate, marshmallows, chewing gum and chocolate. Paradise had finally returned as the shipwreckees prepared to have the best meal since they arrived on the island – no tempers were strained that evening and it was smiles and *bonhomie* all round. And with renewed vigour and excitement they began to make preparations for the second ration run, as two other lads were desperate for their turn as heroes. More lists were drawn up – although the money was much depleted and they had just under $100 left. They also had Jo's twenty-first birthday to look forward to, and they duly began planning for that.

Jo had said that she would like a theme party for her birthday – a sort of James Bond-type affair – which was an idea that all the cast took to with gusto. And Jo was also quietly preparing a James Bond-type scenario for herself – she decided that she would go to the island with Andy and Kev so that she could phone home for her twenty-first. She had to persuade them to take her, which they readily agreed to, and then she

had to swear them to secrecy – and make sure that they meant it. Jo didn't want either of them talking about it and nobody could know until they were well out to sea and it was too late to come back. Her plan was to stow herself away in the canoe while the lads were making their final preparations. It was a simple idea, with a lot of drama involved, and a huge surprise all round. But would it work?

WEEK 9½

Monday *Feeling restless*

Tuesday *Raid crew camp*

Wednesday *Is Jo up to something?*

Thursday *Storms brewing, shelters not up to it*

Friday *Starving*

Saturday *Start planning time capsule*

Sunday *Just a few more days*

Plans moved swiftly to get the lads going on the second ration run. Jody and Tim did a few quick repair jobs on the boat, and the atmosphere around the camp was one of mellowness and goodwill towards everyone. It's surprising what a change of diet and a few marshmallows, not to mention vast quantities of chocolate, can do. It even brought about a rapprochement between Tony and Lucy M. 'I decided to bury the hatchet with Lucy M,' Tony revealed. 'Things have been so dodgy between us for ages, but it would be silly to leave somewhere like this bearing any resentment. I had a chat with her and we talked about what had happened between us and how I wanted to lay it to rest. I wasn't sure how she would respond, but she agreed and we hugged and made up. Maybe I should have done it sooner.'

'We had a great feed and everyone is in good spirits.'
Tony

The laid-back vibe was enhanced by the fact the group decided they no longer needed a leader. The shelter seemed strong, their stint was coming to an end, home was beckoning and all was well with the world. In honour of the first castaway to abandon their tropical paradise, the cast decide to name their non-leader Victoria, and got on with working on their tans and enjoying their final precious days on Nuku.

However, one evening before dinner Tim approached Andy and Kev with a plan – he wanted them to take him to the mainland too. The lads were dumbstruck. They had already agreed to take Jo with them as a special birthday treat and under normal circumstances wouldn't think twice of explaining to Tim that they already had one extra passenger. However, Tim had given them a moral dilemma. He had won his place rightly and properly, and with everybody's agreement, on the first ration run, but he had given it away. Everyone was moved by Tim's gesture at the time, and now the lads had an opportunity to reward him for it – but they had already promised someone else the trip. The two of them went off to La Cosa Nostra to think and talk about it and in the end they felt they had no choice but tell Jo that they were sorry but they couldn't take her after all.

The birthday girl understood all the reasons for their decision, but was bitterly disappointed. She had put such thought into what she could do for her twenty-first and she had been so looking forward to speaking to her parents and to Jay, her boyfriend, on that special day. She resolved to do something else to mark her birthday…

When the lads announced they were taking Tim with them, they couldn't have hoped for a more popular response to their action. Everyone was delighted with them and thrilled for Tim, and so it was with much jubilation that they were waved off for their great adventure. They had also decided between them (because they had to tell Tim about Jo) that they would try and do something really special for her birthday.

As they waved the trio off, the rest of the cast felt that they too should have an adventure. Without any real leader to stop them, they decided that the time had come to really raid the crew camp and see what extra food and refreshments they could garner from there. But a plan was required – one that was sufficiently inventive to take what was left of the crew away

Jo

Best:

Nude sunbathing day –
definitely the best day on
Nuku. The sun was out –
and so were all our
backsides.

D's birthday party –
wearing ivy, singing around
the bonfire, getting drunk
on island rum, collapsing
and being dragged to bed
by Jody and Tim.

Lucy T – big mouth, big
fun, big heart.

Tim's bum – the cutest and
whitest bum on the island.

Escaping from Nuku was
the highlight of being
shipwrecked for me, and a
fantastic ending to the
most amazing time of my
life (so far).

Worst:

The food – it was awful
and I hated it all (apart
from Emma's curry). The
corned beef and rice was
disgusting.

Group meetings – too
many, too often.

The long-drop and digging
it – the long-drop was the
most disgusting thing I
have ever seen – especially
when it was full of flies!
And digging it! Ehhhh! That
shit was green.

Jody's hat – Jody, it just did
nothing for you and made
you look about ten. I
wanted to burn it and to
this day I don't know why I
didn't.

Being homesick, having no
contact at all with home
and missing them all so
much I couldn't even bear
to think about them.

from their camp (the other half of the crew was following the lads to film them).

Over lunch they came up with their great scheme and Emma-Rosa was deputized to lure the crew to the far side of the beach. She immediately went into great performer mode and told them that she needed to tell them something but had to be far enough away from the rest of the cast for them not to suspect anything. So, on a quiet and secluded part of the island, she began her tale of treachery. Tim, Kev and Andy were never going to come back to Nuku, she declared. A few of the cast members had heard them discuss their plans, but didn't want to stop them; however, Emma said that she felt that the crew would want to know what was likely to happen on the mainland. They filmed her conscientiously and did a few re-takes. It was only when she thought her co-conspirators had had enough time to do their worst that Emma burst out laughing and told the crew that she'd just told them a pack of lies!

Retribution followed swiftly. The crew decided to remove both the tarpaulin from the roof and the groundsheet from the floor of the communal shelter. The cast didn't care too much about this at first, as they were thoroughly enjoying the beers, crisps and cola they found in crew camp. Until, that is, they suddenly noticed that storm clouds were gathering and the realization hit them that they had no place to shelter from the rain. Those who had already built their own private shelters checked that everything was storm-proof about them, while the others hurriedly built new shelters. The storm came, and while a few had a sleepless and wet night, most of the ship-wreckees manage to escape from the worst of the rain.

All energies were now involved in making costumes and presents for Jo's party. Lucy T made herself an extravagant affair out of palm leaves rolled up inside mosquito netting with several

tentacles, so that she could go as Octopussy; the others were less ambitious. Jo, however, was the person with the most daring idea – she decided that she was going to use her twenty-first birthday as her chance to escape…

Meanwhile, the lads reached the mainland and decided it was time to party. They abandoned all plans to try and blag their way into staying at a starry hotel. Instead, they headed straight for Ernie's house and, with typical Tongan hospitality, he invited them to stay with him. The three were delighted and decided that what they saved on accommodation they could spend on red wine. They also determined to buy Jo a birthday cake, but before any shopping could take place, and after a shower and a few beers, they unfolded their grand plan to Ernie in order to enlist his help.

What they had in mind was to sell *Victoria* – Jody's carefully mended and constructed little boat – hitch a lift with Ernie back to Nuku and spend all the proceeds on luxuries. They intended their ration run to be done in style. Ernie was delighted with the idea, offered all his help and took them off to a group of fishermen to act as salesman for their boat. It was goodbye *Victoria* and hello good times.

Back on Nuku, another boat arrived, this time bringing an Australian journalist who had come to interview the cast. They all crowded onto the beach to welcome her and then took her off to the main camp for the interviews – all, that is, except for one person. Dawdling behind and pretending to look for shells was the birthday girl, who had at last found a way to realize her plan. With the crew's connivance she had decided to jump island, hi-jack the journalist's boat and head off to freedom. While the cast were being interviewed, Jo collected her belongings and swam out to the boat. And once on board, she headed off towards the mainland.

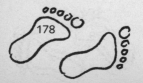

So much was going on that morning – a combination of interviews and final preparations for the party – that nobody noticed Jo's absence until they gathered for lunch. As they were all used to her going off on her own they took no notice at first, but gradually Samara became worried and decided that she was going to find her. She walked all the way around the island, but with no luck; she called out when she got to Jo's hut, but there was no reply. Emma and Blough decided to investigate, and found a letter from Jo explaining what she had done. They brought it back to the group and read it out, to a reaction of pure amazement. Eventually, when they'd

---

Lucy T

Best:

Having my twenty-first birthday on the island and all the effort everybody went to so I had a wicked day, island presents etc.

Having the best bath in the world and being able to swim in it.

The sky – the stars at night were amazing and every night we used to watch the sunsets together, which was wicked, and they were the most amazing sunsets ever!

Being the loudest person on the island. I was so loud that I was able to be heard from the neighbouring island, which was a half-hour swim away!

Corny as it sounds, the people I met made the whole experience and I've made some brilliant friends. Everyone rocked big styley!

Worst:

Jo leaving the island on her birthday (and I had spent a week making my costume, but we had the party anyway) without telling us. It was horrible, it felt like someone had died. I missed her so much.

Leaving my boyfriend, family and friends was majorly horrible – knowing I was doing something which would change me considerably and would be such an important part of my life and they wouldn't be there to share it with me.

The chickens being killed and eaten was a major low point of the whole thing, because I loved looking after them and my favourite chicken, Ethel, had the best red rubbery comb on top of her head EVER. She was a headbanging chicken!

People hogging the camera and trying over-desperately to get into every possible shot was a nightmare, and I actually felt embarrassed for them for being so desperate in the end – S.A.D.

The toilet was absolutely the most minging thing ever imaginable. It was swarming with flies the size of mice, which used to crawl all over us all the time. Re-digging the long-drop was the worst thing, and it made us all retch because it heaved with maggots and it stank for Britain!

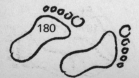

found their voices, some of the cast cheered at the audacity and style of the whole thing. However, Lucy T and Samara were inconsolable – and so was Stuart, who wept in front of everyone.

When the lads returned with Ernie a few hours later, they were met with long faces and shocked expressions. The excitement of their return had been much diminished by the sadness that accompanied Jo's departure. However, the wine, Ernie's smiles and the decision to go ahead with the party boosted the atmosphere tremendously. Emma-Rosa, back at the helm in the kitchen, made one of her special Thai green curries.

'I know when I go home I'll miss this place.'
Tim

Strangely, while there were luxuries and presents for everyone, there was something almost elegiac about the evening. All of the group began to reflect on their stay in paradise and discuss whether it was the chance of a lifetime and worth the hardships and deprivations. Of course, they agreed that none of them would have missed it for anything.

Earlier in the week, before he had gone on the ration run, Tim had gone to the hut-cam with a message that he had been wanting to deliver for weeks, and around the campfire this particular evening the rest of the cast wished to emulate it. Tim told the camera: 'It's hard to realize just how lucky we are to be here. I really wish I had a camera to capture the beauty of the place, but at least we will have the programme when we

go back. Ever since I got here I've wanted to thank someone for this opportunity; it's so perfect and so different.'

But time was running out and the idyll was soon to come to an end. One of the castaways' last acts as a group was to put together a time capsule to bury on the island. Each member of the cast contributed something – such as a poem, a bracelet, a piece of fishing wire or a shell – which was to remind the island forever of the shipwreckees. As for the latter, they knew some part of them would always remain on the tropical paradise. A little ceremony was held, a hole was dug and something of *Shipwrecked* became part of Nuku.

Finally, the last day dawned – but, typically, it was overcast, and the group began to wonder if their departure, like their arrival, would be delayed. Disconsolately, they waited by the beach, scanning the horizon for the first sign of a boat, but any they saw went off in different directions to fish. Their excitement turned to dread – everything was packed, there were no rations left, their huts were almost destroyed; what would they do if the boat failed to show? The boat finally arrived late in the afternoon, but because of the tides and the current it couldn't come into land, so the castaways had to swim out to it, with their belongings. A few sad faces, a couple of drowned rats and many chattering teeth later, they turned to wave goodbye to their own private paradise. They hugged each other for comfort, but home and loved ones were beckoning.

En route to Pangaimotu, the resort island they'd visited on their way out to Nuku all those weeks ago, Ernie performed his own little ceremony of farewell. He told the cast stories about the islands and the people who had visited from far and wide down the centuries. And then, while presenting them with wooden carvings with their names engraved on each one,

he told them that they would always have a place in his heart. There were more tears, more hugs and more regretful glances back to the exquisite speck of sun, sand and sea that was their home for nine and a half weeks. But now life – real life – awaited.

JO'S DIARY

Yesterday I made the decision that I was going to escape from the island either before or on my twenty-first birthday – anything after being a waste of time – which means at the most I have two days here. I came to the decision after a day realizing I don't want to be here any longer, involved in all the petty arguments and silly discussions floating around the cast camp. I don't want to leave the island – especially on days like today, when it is at its most beautiful – but then again, I want to do Nuku island justice and leave with my most wonderful memories still intact. As I have said before, escaping from here will not be escaping from the island, it will be escaping from the way I am feeling, and if this island has taught me anything, it is to be strong and follow my heart. Remaining here for another eight days would not be following my heart.

As strange as this sounds, tonight must be one of the most 'lived' nights I have ever experienced. Everything round me is alive, moving and giving off the most intense and awe-inspiring energy – including myself. The sea is lashing calmly but noisily against the shore. The wind is whistling past my ears and through my hair flapping at the written pages of my journal. The leaves behind me and above are dancing; the crickets are singing and the sky above me is alive with light and movement, lightning and thunder. And I am alive at the thought of leaving this island in a day's time on my own. I am alive because I have lived the whole experience the way I wanted to – I never lost sight of who I was, I never tried to be anyone but me. And now I am leaving as me. As Joanne, who

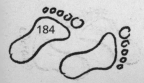

weaved non-stop for two weeks; as 'Joanne the Blonde'; the one who built her own shelter and the one who wanted to be on her own and to distance herself from the group. I am leaving here as Joanne, the one who had an amazing time here, but knew when it was time for her to leave – and was not afraid to leave.

Today has been one of the craziest days ever, and a day I will remember for the rest of my life. This morning I woke up on Nuku island after a good night's sleep and as a twenty-one-year-old. The crew came and told me all was well with their plan and that the boat would be arriving within the hour. My bag was put into the dustbin liners and taken down to the beach disguised as rubbish, and then the whole group met the journalist off the beach and walked her up to camp. I then made the excuse to get my waterproof jacket as it was starting to rain – grabbed my stuff, made sure that nobody was watching, and ran into the water. I then swam as hard as I could towards the boat, threw my stuff on and hid. The camera crew were on board and on the beach to catch all the action, and me panting as I got on the boat and lighting up as I realized I had made it – I had escaped! No more group! No more silly arguments and mind-numbing discussions. No more stupid group meetings… It's back to doing things that actually matter. It's back to doing things which mean something, relationships which matter and are not forced. Back to real life and real living. I am so glad I had the experience. It has meant so much to me and I have had a fantastic time. I am just so glad that it is over and done with now – and I am glad I left in this fantastic way on this fantastic day.

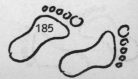

'FROM ME TO ALL OF YOU'
BY SAMARA MILFORD

We seventeen were all once part of Nuku Island
Once part of each other
Now our time is over
And we must return to our homes
And whether how far or how near
I know that each one of us
Is inside the hearts of sixteen others
Whether in love, hate or friendship
Or all three
It is something we will all be joined by
We have become close in a way
That we may never have dreamed of
That seventeen complete strangers
Could find love for each other
And now that we return to our lives
This experience is something that is etched
In our hearts and in our minds
Never to be erased
But with time
Cherished and polished and gleaming
With all that was good
And it will become a pearl of wisdom
That we can share with others
But it will always be our space in time
That we were the strongest
Each one of us could be
When we were Shipwrecked.

HOME AGAIN

And so, like all good things, the sojourn on the island – the chance of a glimpse of paradise – came to an end. By the time it finished, the experience had started to pall for the fourteen remaining shipwreckees. They'd been counting the days till their return for some time, and thoughts of friends and families were now at the forefront of the their minds, not shoved to the back, as they had been when there were still so many weeks to go.

New friendships had been formed; new enmities had lost their initial aggression. However, there was still tension in the air – the camp was split, and matters weren't helped by the uncertain weather, which had become hot, humid and stormy. The food remained monotonously the same, give or take a few treats from the mainland and what could be nicked from the crew camp. Everyone was bored, all the books had been read, those who wanted to had built their own huts, and they'd grown weary of collecting shells from the beach and making them into jewellery.

It was time to go home. Back to watching television, instead of being filmed for a television programme. Back to people, traffic, mobile phones, pubs, pizzas and roast dinners, real beds, flushing lavatories and everything on tap. Just below the veneer of ennui was a palpable excitement – which is why the entire cast were fed up that their departure day was delayed by a late boat and bad weather. To top it all, they had to swim to the boat, getting both themselves and their clothes soaking wet, so leaving was nearly as nearly as traumatic as the arrival had been.

As they turned around for the last view of the island that had

187

been their home for the last nine and a half weeks, many of the shipwreckees were so choked that they couldn't speak. 'My emotions were running too high,' Blough confesses. When asked what were the best things about being on the island, most of the cast put the island itself high on the list – and that's in spite of the mosquitoes, the tropical storms, the food and the long-drop. Tony thinks he was the only one who didn't want to leave at the end. 'It was the most amazing experience and like nothing that I've ever done before,' he admits. 'I've travelled to China, Tibet and Australia, often on my own… more so than anyone else in the group, but this was something else. This was something wonderful. I was really depressed for about two weeks after getting back.'

And all this, even though his time on the island had been tainted by rows and accusations. 'I was in many ways used to survival expeditions from my travels but this was social experiment too,' Tony acknowledges. 'To this day I don't truly understand what happened with the Aussie girls or with Lucy M. With the former they may have found us crude, maybe immature and silly, but we soon made up. But Lucy was something different and I think the cameras stirred quite a bit of it too. I thought her saying I had a on-screen and an off-screen persona was a cowardly way to attack me and it really upset me. In the end I became paranoid as to how I was perceived in the group, terrified of being thought of as the Nasty Nick character.'

And boy, did he learn from his stay on Nuku. 'Paradise as it was, [the experience] was emotionally harrowing. It left me much more tolerant and appreciative of people's quirks and differences and I learnt that I was not as tough as I thought I was, but neither was I as emotionally cold as I thought.' Tony admits that he would go back to Nuku tomorrow, but that he'd take a different list of luxuries: 'Next time, no guitar, which I broke on the fourth day, irreparably – you could say I smashed it in true rock and roll fashion, but that wouldn't be quite the whole truth!'

With just one exception, the entire cast felt their stay on a deserted South Sea island had been the chance of a lifetime, an opportunity to find out about themselves as much as about other people. Jo, the last escapee, thought it had been the best experience of her life. 'I grew up a lot and really surprised myself,' she explains. 'Until I went to Nuku I hated being on my own, and in fact was never on my own. At university I either lived with my sister or stayed with my boyfriend – in fact, if I lived anywhere it was in my car. I so surprised myself, because I spent a lot of time on my own and loved it.'

Part of the reason she adapted so well, she thinks, was because she always kept herself busy – she helped put the camp together, spent days weaving for the structure, then made mattresses for everybody before setting about making presents of shell jewellery and bags for island birthdays and for friends at home. And that was before she made her own hut, which she did completely on her own, cutting down trees and weaving palms for the roof. 'It also made me aware that I could get on with everyone and I really respected them,' she reflects. 'Of course we had rows, but really they were over silly, unimportant things. But it was sensible really, 'cos we chose safe subjects to argue about, so we avoided being really hurtful to each other.'

The one castaway who felt she'd learnt little from the experience was Lucy M, although now she's back, she has found that some of her innermost thought processes have been subverted by the experience! 'I hated all that group thing out there,' she comments. 'I was never group-orientated. I went there for me, not for anyone else, and had no intention of becoming part of a cell. And yet, now I am more group aware

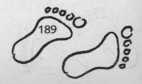

189

than before. For instance, there is someone in the house I live in who is about to be pushed out, and yet before we [evict them] I want to call a group meeting!' And while Lucy admits that she had nothing in common with the other people on the island, she allows that she began to relax and enjoy herself much more towards the end of the stay: 'I got really homesick very quickly, so it took a long time for me to even begin to enjoy it. The last week was great because I moved in with Stuart and Lisa and we had a good time.' On her return, Lucy M made a conscious decision not to contact anyone for a couple of weeks, but an e-mail from Lucy T got her back into the swing of being a shipwreckee, and in no time at all she was getting drunk with old arch-enemy Tony!

Even tough guy Dharma accepts that he underwent a quantum change in attitude over his time on the island. 'My personal motives were basically to stay the ten weeks and to do it right,' he states. 'It's an amazing thing to do in your life and I was determined to have no regrets from the experience, and I had none. The disparity between the Brits and Aussies was a little daunting, but I just included it in the overall challenge and I was never really disappointed [or] disillusioned... although there were times when I thought these people were going to drive me mad!

'But my perceptions changed about everybody a lot and in the end all the guys turned out to be really great blokes. Tim was one of the guys who wasn't such a lad, which made it easier for me to get on with him, I think. He was older than most of us and I appreciated him because he obviously knew who he was more than some of the others. After my birthday present I thought he was bloody champion.'

The other Aussies also came away with warm views about the Brits, and a strong sense of themselves. Lisa agrees that she

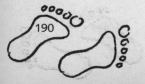

has learnt, 'heaps about myself. I learned that I am strong and not afraid of a challenge. I also learned that tolerance and acceptance of others is imperative if you want to live in peace.'

Larissa says she will be forever grateful for the quality thinking time the weeks on the island gave her. 'I wanted to get away from the city, the rat race and society.' Moreover, she and her boyfriend Aaron were going through a few difficult patches prior to her jaunt to Nuku, which they both needed time to consider. On her return they chose to part: 'We decided that we are better off as friends. My life is definitely better for the [*Shipwrecked*] experience, and I do not regret a day of it. It put everything into perspective and I've never been so motivated. My friends and family are closer to me than ever, and my career has never been so good.'

If Larissa was disappointed about anything, it was the cameras. 'Disillusion set in when I realized that everything we did and said was going to be exploited for television,' she confesses. 'I would love to do it again some time – but playing by my rules and without the cameras. Some friends are talking about doing it in Thailand next year… so, maybe.'

Not only did the castaways learn how to cope with lack of privacy, boring food and mosquitoes, they also learned how to build, weave, kill chickens, catch fish and make fires. For some there were personal fears to be conquered. Jody, often voted the most popular man on Nuku, had a phobia about sea water. Not a good thing if you've volunteered to live on a small island surrounded by the largest ocean on the planet. But he was determined to deal with his fear. 'I was stung by a jellyfish as a child and was terrified of the sea,' he reveals. 'For years I would not swim out of my depth. On Nuku there was no way around it, so I just made myself go do it. Within two weeks I was swimming out to the reef and catching fish, and by the end of our stay I was one of the strongest swimmers on the island. We had been given a chance in a million, I really couldn't let anything spoil it.' And this is the guy who came with a fear of sea water and ended up swimming after sharks!

Stuart's perceptions were also changed by his sojourn. 'Before I went I never looked at the sky, I hardly noticed it – and now I can't stop looking at it,' he marvels. 'But it was like everything on that island. I kept getting these extraordinary visual rushes – the beaches, the skies and the reef, it was fantastic, like living through an amazing David Attenborough film. I really miss the beauty.' He goes on to explain that he not only learnt to understand the beauty of nature, but also to appreciate the beauty of mod cons. Ordinary everyday things – like fresh water and a toaster.

For all of the castaways, the paradise isle of Nuku will eventually take a backseat in their lives. However, every so often a movie, a moonlit sky, or even a television programme will bring it sharply back into focus, along with memories of the dramatic effect it had on their lives. It will be an experience they will tell their children and grandchildren about. And somewhere, there will be a video of them when they were young and carefree… and fed up at having to eat another plate of rice and beetroot! But for one member of this second *Shipwrecked* cast, going back is an absolute must. Before leaving Tonga, Beth let Ernie – their teacher and provider – into a secret, and when she arrived home it was one of the first things she told her mother. 'When I get married I am definitely going back,' she reveals. 'Ernie knows and will expect me, and my mum says I had better start saving now.'

So after all, it was more than just paradise – for some it was also the perfect setting for romance. And the next time Beth sets foot on the sands of Nuku, she'll only have one other person to share the island with…